PResented to:

_____

PResented by:

_____

date:

_____

LiVE
like a
JESUS
Freak

LiVE
like a JESUS
Freak

Spend Today as If It Were Your Last

dcTalk

BETHANY HOUSE PUBLISHERS
MINNEAPOLIS, MINNESOTA

Live Like a Jesus Freak:
Spend Today as If It Were Your Last
Copyright © 2001 by BETHANY HOUSE PUBLISHERS

Original content written by Angie Kiesling, Sanford, Florida

Published by Bethany House Publishers
11400 Hampshire Avenue South
Bloomington, Minnesota 55438

Bethany House Publishers is a division of
Baker Publishing Group, Grand Rapids, Michigan.

Printed in the United States of America

Library of Congress Cataloging-in-Publication Data

DC Talk (Musical Group).
    Live like a Jesus Freak; spend today as if it were your last / by dcTalk.
    p. cm.
    ISBN 1-57778-208-9 (pbk)
  1. Christian life. I. Title.
    2001

2002277044

Dedicated
to . . .

All THOSE who
will pick up
their CROSSES
daily and
follow JESUS

freak \`fr_k\

n. [origin unknown] (1563)

1. A sudden and odd or seemingly pointless idea or turn of the mind.

2. A seemingly capricious action or event.

3. A strange, abnormal, or unusual person or thing.

4. An ardent enthusiast.[1]

"You're just
JEALOUS
because I'm a
real FREAK
and you have to
wear a MASK."

—The Penguin, from *Batman Returns*

TaBle of ConTeNts

How to Live like a JESUS Freak

A Word Before We Start

A few years back, *Jesus Freaks* was published, and the world was impacted. People around the world read this book and made decisions to turn their back on "life as usual" and become what many call "Jesus Freaks."

"Jesus Freak" started off as a derogatory term for people who were radical in the way they followed Jesus. True believers, however, took it as a compliment—to be labeled a Jesus Freak meant others saw a difference in your life, and that—perhaps—Jesus was beginning to mess with their lives as well. And that is a good thing.

Throughout this book, you will see the term Jesus Freak used often. When you do, think of a Jesus Freak not as someone who is perfect, or even close to perfect. A Jesus Freak is simply one who knows he or she cannot be perfect without God's incredible grace and mercy, and daily seeks those two gifts. A Jesus Freak has chosen to leave this life behind and seek the abundant life God promises. This is a choice that is made daily, and some days are better than others. But still, God forgives.

If you have not yet made the decision to leave all and follow Jesus, keep reading. Perhaps once you have tasted of the banquet our Host sets out each day, featuring His strength instead of your weakness, hope in place of hopelessness, and peace, mercy, and justice in overflowing amounts, you will also decide to become a Jesus Freak.

Introduction

If you're reading this book, you must want to live a radical life for Jesus. Why else would you bother to open these pages? In the following ten chapters you'll delve deeper into what it means to be a Jesus Freak. You'll learn why standing out from the crowd is a good thing. Most of all, you'll catch a glimpse of the fact that as a Jesus Freak you're in good company—the very best, in fact.

Do you see what this means—all these pioneers who blazed the way, all these veterans cheering us on? It means we'd better get on with it. Strip down, start running—and never quit! No extra spiritual fat, no parasitic sins. Keep your eyes on Jesus, who both began and finished this race we're in. Study how he did it. Because he never lost sight of where he was headed—that exhilarating finish in and with God—he could put up with anything along the way: cross, shame, whatever. And now he's there, in the place of honor, right alongside God.

—HEBREWS 12:1-2, THE MESSAGE

One word of warning: This book is not a prescription for a safe, comfortable life. Nor is it a syllabus for Spirituality 101. When Jesus crashed onto the human scene 2,000 years ago, He turned the world upside down. The same Man who turned over the moneychangers' tables—and conventional ideas of how to reach God—is still in the business of wreaking Godly havoc on people's lives. Are you ready to take the plunge?

Before you became a Jesus Freak, you might have been known as bold and wild, a fearless person with a "bring it on!" attitude. Now maybe you want to channel that energy into a sold-out relationship with God, but you're not sure how to go about it. Or maybe you were the quiet, shy type, always feeling as if you were on the outside looking in. Now that Jesus rules your life, you're ready to move off the fringes and into the fray.

Jesus never promised that being His follower would be easy. Quite the opposite, in fact. Look at His words:

If anyone would come after me, he must deny himself and take up his cross and follow me. For whoever wants to save his life will lose it, but whoever loses his life for me will find it.

—MATTHEW 16:24-25

Toward the end of His life on earth, Jesus set out on the road to Jerusalem with His disciples. As they journeyed through dusty villages on the way to the Holy City, they bumped into would-be Jesus Freaks along the way. One man told Jesus he would follow Him anywhere—but first he needed to bury his father. Jesus' reply seems harsh when we read it today, but He was deliberately making a point: "Let the dead bury their own dead, but you go and proclaim the kingdom of God."

Still another said, "I will follow You, Lord, but first let me go back and say good-bye to my family." Using a cultural image the man would understand, Jesus told him that no one who puts his hand to the plow and looks back is fit to serve God. In other words, you're either in this or you're not—no turning back.

What about you? Is something holding you back from all-out commitment to Christ? Before you wade into the pages of this book, dig deep into your soul—the real you. Are you ready to forsake all and follow Him? Are you ready to . . .

Live
like a
JESUS
Freak

"While we may not be called to martyr our lives, we must martyr our way of life. We must put our selfish ways to death and march to a different beat. Then the world will see Jesus."

—MICHAEL TAIT OF DC TALK[2]

ChaPter ONE

Believe

like a

JESUS
Freak

On the dc Talk album, *Jesus Freak,* author and speaker Brennan Manning draws this conclusion. "The single greatest cause of atheism in the world today is Christians who acknowledge Jesus with their lips, then walk out the door and deny HIm by their lifestyle. That is what an unbelieving world simply finds unbelievable."

Everybody despises a fake. If you wear a façade, sooner or later the real you will show through. When it finally does, you'd better be prepared to deal with the consequences! That's what happened to the religious leaders of Jesus' day. They paraded around wearing holy-looking robes. They made a show of their long-winded, pious-sounding prayers. And they always snagged a front-row seat at key events. After all, they were the big cheeses, the spiritual elite of their day—and everybody knew it.

Jesus saw through the Pharisees' façade. He blasted them for their fake religiosity, comparing them to sheep in wolves' clothing and a pit of snakes. When it comes to religion, it seems the twenty-first century is no different from the first century.

It takes
courage
to **live**
a **BOLD,**
passionate
life for
Christ
in today's
world.

While phoniness earns our disrespect and anger, truthfulness is respected, even when it's unpopular. As a Jesus Freak, you probably already know there will be times when you will stand out from the crowd because of your beliefs. Maybe the popular crowd laughs at you; perhaps your old friends avoid you. Jesus told us to expect that—it comes with the territory when we deny our old lifestyle and "take up our cross" to follow Him. Even though you may suffer ridicule, deep down those same people may respect you. The reality is that even popular culture admires courage. Courage in action is a common movie theme:

A young woman in a mental hospital stands up to the testing of the psych-ward bully, earning her grudging respect and even her friendship in the end. (Girl, Interrupted)

A famous author-turned-recluse befriends a young urban male, teaching him the finer points of writing. When his cherished anonymity is threatened, he chooses to go public to save his young friend's reputation. (Finding Forrester)

Two lifelong friends fight side by side in World War II. Although they both love the same woman, one friend takes a bullet for the other and gives up the possibility of a life with her. (Pearl Harbor)

It takes courage to live a bold, passionate life for Christ in today's world. In our gut, we all know nothing less will do. But you may be asking, "How can I consistently live what I believe?" It's a fair question. The temptation to cave in to the peer pressure around you is a daily battle, and the messages sent by the media aren't exactly growing tamer by the day. How can Jesus Freaks maintain their integrity? How can Jesus Freaks do more than talk about their faith? As an earlier generation used to say, how can Jesus Freaks "walk the talk"?

As St. Francis is known for saying, "Always tell of God's love. If necessary, use words."

"What Will People Do When They Find Out It's True?"

It was the late 1930s, and Hitler's war machine was ravaging one European country after another. Corrie ten Boom, a single Dutch woman who lived a quiet life above her father's watch shop, was about to have her life shaken to the core. As the Gestapo moved in to the town of Haarlem, the narrow, creaking old house harbored not only Corrie's close-knit family but also a secret chamber—a hiding place for Jews hoping to escape the Nazi concentration camps.

Recalling the day in January 1937 when she, her sister, and her father celebrated the watch shop's 100th anniversary, Corrie wrote in her book *The Hiding Place:* "How could we have guessed as we sat there . . . that in place of memories we were about to be given adventure such as we had never dreamed of? Adventure and anguish, horror and heaven were just around the corner, and we did not know. Oh Father! Betsie! If I had known, would I have gone ahead? Could I have done the things I did?"

As the Nazis invaded Holland, the ten Boom family operated an "underground" operation that fed, clothed, and housed Jews—and often spirited them away to safety. When the Nazis discovered their scheme, Corrie and Betsie were shipped off to prison and eventually landed in Ravensbrück, one of the most notorious concentration camps.

With the help of a smuggled Bible, the sisters dispensed hope and the gospel to their fellow inmates, and gradually watched a divine pattern unfold. Before she died in Ravensbrück, Betsie told Corrie, "Your whole life has been a training ground for the work you are doing here in prison—and the work you will do afterward." After her release from Ravensbrück, Corrie traveled the globe as a self-described "tramp for the Lord," sharing her story with thousands. One day, as she spoke at a church service in post-war Munich, she saw a face she recognized—a face that made her stomach clench with hatred. It was the guard who had stood watch over the shower room door at Ravensbrück. And now here he was making his way to the front, his eyes on her!

The man—who could not have recognized her—stopped in front of Corrie and thrust out his hand. "How grateful I am for your message, Fräulein. To think that, as you say, He has washed my sins away!"

Corrie froze. This was a test, and she knew it—was her faith real, or was she just paying lip service to God? Jesus had said, *"Love your enemies . . . pray for those which despitefully use you"* (Matthew 5:44 KJV). Sending up a silent prayer for supernatural forgiveness, she extended her hand in return. As she did, "the most incredible thing happened," she writes. "From my shoulder along my arm and through my hand a current seemed to pass from me to him, while into my heart sprang a love for this stranger that almost overwhelmed me. And so I discovered that it is not on our forgiveness any more than on our goodness that the world's healing hinges, but on His. When He tells us to love our enemies, He gives, along with the command, the love itself."[3]

Do you have the courage to offer love when it may be thrown back in your face?

Are you willing to share your story—the story of how you became a Jesus Freak—even if it means people may laugh and walk away?

God fuels us with supernatural power to live and love the way Christ did when He walked the earth.

Strong Faith in the Dry Seasons

Loneliness. Depression. A "who-cares" attitude toward God. We all feel like this from time to time, but as Jesus Freaks we put pressure on ourselves—and others—to pick ouselves up. *Jesus is still Lord, right?* we tell ourselves, trying to prop up our emotions with a self-induced pep talk.

God FUELS us **with** supernatural **power** to LIVE and LOVE the **way** Christ did when He WALKED the **earth.**

The Bible, and history itself, abounds with stories of Jesus Freaks who faced their share of hard times. What was their secret to going the distance? How did they stay true to Christ in the long haul? Listen to the words of one famous Jesus Freak who experienced high "highs" and low "lows":

> *Save me, God!*
> *I am about to drown.*
> *I am sinking deep in the mud,*
> *and my feet are slipping.*
> *I am about to be swept under by a*
> *   mighty flood.*
> *I am worn out from crying,*
> *and my throat is dry.*
> *I have waited for you*
> *till my eyes are blurred.*
> —PSALM 69:1-3 CEV

David wasn't timid about airing his troubles and frustrations with God—he did not try to hide what he was feeling. At the same time, he recognized that his strength and hope could only be found in the Lord. Two psalms later we hear him proclaiming:

> *I will never give up hope*
> *or stop praising you.*
> *All day long I will tell*
> *the wonderful things you do*
> *to save your people.*
> *But you have done much more*
> *than I could possibly know . . .*
> *You made me suffer a lot,*
> *but you will bring me*

back from this deep pit
and give me new life.

—Psalm 71:14-15,20 CEV

"Fits of depression come over most of us," the great nineteenth-century preacher Charles Spurgeon once told his students. "The strong are not always vigorous, the joyous are not always happy."

Spurgeon sure knew what he was talking about. Even though he is considered one of history's greatest preachers, he was prone to agonizing periods of depression. He suffered a horrible bout of discouragement when he was only twenty-two years old. Frustrated that his congregation had outgrown its building, Spurgeon booked a large concert hall in London. As he stood to speak on Sunday morning, he said, "We shall be gathered together tonight where an unprecedented mass of people will assemble, perhaps from idle curiosity, to hear God's Word; see what God can do, just when a cloud is falling on the head of him whom God has raised up to preach to you."

That night 12,000 people packed Surrey Hall; another 10,000 overflowed into the gardens. Instigated by the false cry of "Fire! Fire!" the crowd bolted in panic, trampling seven people to death. Spurgeon collapsed from shock and was taken to a friend's house to recover. He remained in seclusion for weeks, begging God to reveal the *why* behind what had happened. Finally, while meditating on Scripture, his spirit and health were revived.

Incredibly, that disaster was the catalyst for Charles Spurgeon's overnight fame as a preacher of the gospel.

The verse that triggered Spurgeon's restoration were these simple words from Philippians 2:10: *". . . that at the name of Jesus every knee should bow, in heaven and on earth and under the earth."*

Like the love relationship between a man and a woman, our love for God will go through ups and downs. That's only natural. God made us who we are, and the Bible says He "remembers that we are clay." He knows we sometimes have doubts and go through times of uncertainty. King David and Corrie ten Boom went through such times. But be courageous. Even if you can't see or feel God at a crucial moment, know that He has promised to never leave you. And He always keeps His promises.

How can you consistently live what you believe?
How can people know from your life that Jesus
is real?

When your faith wavers or discouragement piles up
on you, where do you turn?

What three things can you say or do the next time
you enter a "dry season" in your life as a Jesus
Freak? (Hint: Check out Psalm 71 again.)

Jesus Freaks Around You Now

The Cigarette Sermons
Linh Dao, Vietnam, 1991

Four police officers suddenly burst into ten-year-old Linh Dao's home. They forced her father, an underground pastor in North Vietnam, to remain seated while the authorities ransacked the home, searching for Bibles.

"I remember when the police came," Linh Dao recalls. "They searched around the house all of that morning and asked many different questions. It was scary to talk to the policemen, but I knew what they were looking for, so I concentrated and tried my best not to be scared or nervous." As the police questioned her parents, Linh courageously hid some of the Bibles in her school knapsack.

When the police asked her about the contents of the knapsack, Linh simply replied, "It is books for children."

Linh Dao's father was arrested that day and sentenced to seven years of re-education through hard labor.

"When the policemen decided to take my dad away, all of my family knelt down and prayed. I prayed first, then my sister, then my mom, and last of all, my dad. I prayed that my dad would have peace and remain healthy and that my family would survive these hard times. We were all crying, but I told myself I have to face what's happening now."

Word quickly spread about the arrest, and neighbor children began to ask Linh about the crimes her father had been arrested for. She told her friends, "My father is not a criminal. He is a Christian, and I am proud of him for not wavering in his faith!"

As each day passed, Linh Dao made a mark on her wooden bookcase as she prayed for her father. She remembers, "I cried almost every single night, because I worried how my father was doing in prison and how the policemen were treating him.

"Before my dad was in prison, I was just a child. I didn't need to worry about anything. It was a lot different after my dad left. My mind got older very quickly. I told my sister that we had to help Mom do the work around the house, so she could continue to do my dad's work in the church.

"I prayed every day and every night. My faith grew very fast. I knew one thing that I had to concentrate on, and that was spending time learning from the Bible so when I grew up, I could be like my dad, sharing and preaching. When I think about this, I feel my heart burning inside me, pushing me, telling me this is the right thing to do."

Finally, after more than a year, Linh, her mother, and her sister were able to visit their father in prison. When they reached the compound, they were separated by a chain-link fence. Linh quickly discovered that she could squeeze into the prison yard through a chained gate. She ran to her father and hugged him tightly. The guards watched the little girl but, surprisingly, left her alone. *What harm can a little girl do?* they must have thought.

Little did they know! Armed with innocence and a childlike faith, children are a secret weapon against the kingdom of Satan. During that first visit to her father's prison, Linh was able to smuggle him a pen, which he used to write scriptures and sermons on cigarette paper. These "cigarette sermons" traveled from cell to cell and were instrumental in bringing many prisoners to Christ.

Linh Dao's prayers were answered. Her father was released early, before he had served all seven years of his sentence. "It was a big surprise when I came home from school one day and saw my dad had been released from prison. I ran and then gave him a big hug. We were so happy. I was proud of my family, and I wanted to yell and let the whole world know that I wasn't scared of anything, because God always protects each step I go in my life."

Linh Dao is now a teenager. She wants to follow in the footsteps of her father and be a preacher of the gospel of Jesus Christ. She knows firsthand the dangers of sharing her faith in Communist Vietnam and remains determined to obey Christ rather than men. In spite of a "grim future," she spends her time in intense Bible study.[4]

Don't underestimate what you—as one person—can do. God will work through anyone—of any age—who is submitted to Him, to accomplish His will on earth. One man or woman willing to obey God can change the destiny of millions.

Jesus Freaks in the Bible

Jesus Freaks Hall of Fame

Long before sports associations created halls of fame for their star players, God had one of His own. Listed in Hebrews 11, the "Faith Hall of Fame" gives an account of men and women who had the kind of faith Jesus said His Father is looking for. Here's a brief rundown of the Faith Hall of Famers and what they did to deserve a place in the biblical "Who's Who of Jesus Freaks" (Scripture verses taken from THE MESSAGE).

- Abel: *By an act of faith, Abel brought a better sacrifice to God than Cain. It was what he believed, not what he brought, that made the difference.*

- Enoch: *By an act of faith, Enoch skipped death completely . . . We know on the basis of reliable testimony that before he was taken "he pleased God." It's impossible to please God apart from faith. And why? Because anyone who wants to approach God must believe both that he exists and that he cares enough to respond to those who seek him.*

- Noah: *By faith, Noah built a ship in the middle of dry land. He was warned about something he couldn't see, and acted on what he was told.*

- Abraham: *By an act of faith, Abraham said yes to God's call to travel to an unknown place that would become his home. When he left he had no idea where he was going.*

- Sarah: *By faith, barren Sarah was able to become pregnant, old woman as she was at the time, because she believed the One who made a promise would do what he said.*

- Isaac: *By an act of faith, Isaac reached into the future as he blessed Jacob and Esau.*

- Jacob: *By an act of faith, Jacob on his deathbed blessed each of Joseph's sons in turn, blessing them with God's blessing, not his own.*

- Joseph: *By an act of faith, Joseph, while dying, prophesied the exodus of Israel, and made arrangements for his own burial.*

- Moses: *By faith, Moses, when grown, refused the privileges of the Egyptian royal house. He chose a hard life with God's people rather than an opportunistic soft life of sin with the oppressors. He valued suffering in the Messiah's camp far greater than Egyptian wealth because he was looking ahead, antici-pating the payoff.*

- Rahab: *By an act of faith, Rahab, the Jericho harlot, welcomed the [Israelite] spies and escaped the destruction that came on those who refused to trust God.*

Here the writer of Hebrews seems at a loss for
words. He then writes,

*I could go on and on, but I've run out of time.
There are so many more—Gideon, Barak, Samson,
Jephthah, David, Samuel, the prophets . . . Through acts
of faith, they toppled kingdoms, made justice work, took
the promises for themselves. They were protected from
lions, fires, and sword thrusts, turned disadvantage to
advantage, won battles, routed alien armies. Women
received their loved ones back from the dead. There
were those who, under torture, refused to give in and go
free, preferring something better: resurrection. Others
braved abuse and whips, and, yes, chains and dungeons.
We have stories of those who were stoned, sawed in two,
murdered in cold blood; stories of vagrants wandering
the earth in animal skins, homeless, friendless, power-
less—the world didn't deserve them!—making their
way as best they could on the cruel edges of the world.*

*Not one of these people, even though their lives of
faith were exemplary, got their hands on what was
promised. God had a better plan for us: that their faith
and our faith would come together, to make one
completed whole, their lives of faith not complete apart
from ours.*

—HEBREWS 11:32-40 THE MESSAGE

ChaPter **TWO**

Pray
like a
JESUS
Freak

Pray all of the time.

—1 THESSALONIANS 5:17 THE MESSAGE

It was late afternoon on February 26, 1968, and James Stegalls was far from his home—he was serving a tour of duty in Vietnam. The deadly quiet of the jungle was suddenly broken by a piercing, metallic scream. The unmistakable sound of a rocket shooting toward him made his heart thud in his chest. A friend shoved him into a foxhole, and he braced for the explosion, but only a surreal silence followed. The fuse had malfunctioned.

Stegalls crouched in the foxhole for five hours as the battle raged. In his shirt pocket was a Gideons' New Testament. With shaking fingers, he took out the New Testament and began reading Matthew. When his eyes fell on Matthew 18:19-20, he felt a strange peace and somehow knew things would be all right.

Years later, back in the States, Stegalls visited his grandmother. She told him a story he had never heard before—how one night she feared for him and prayed all night for his life. She read Matthew 18:19-20: "Again, I tell you that if two of you on earth agree about anything you ask for, it will be done for you by my Father in heaven. For where two or three come together in my name, there am I with them." After reading the passage, she had called her Sunday school teacher, and the two of them prayed for James.

Stegalls' grandmother then opened her Bible and showed him the date: February 26, 1968.[5]

Prayer is power. It's supernatural firepower that wages war in the invisible realm—the reality that's beyond this temporary world we live in. William Booth, the founder of the Salvation Army, said, "Pray as if everything depended upon your prayer." The eighteenth-century English author William Law said, "There is nothing that makes us love a [person] so much as praying for him." And the Word of God says: "Confess your sins to each other and pray for each other so God can heal you. When a believing person prays, great things happen" (James 5:16 NCV). This same verse in another version reads, "The effective, fervent prayer of a righteous man avails much" (NKJV).

That's an odd word, *fervent*—one that's not found in the vocabulary of most people today. What does it mean to pray fervently? Webster defines *fervent* as "marked by great intensity of feeling."[6] That pretty much sums up how Jesus Freaks are called to pray. Jesus had harsh words for the spiritual leaders of His day because they prayed long, repetitious, passionless prayers that didn't spring from the heart. Instead, they said their prayers for show, to let everyone know how "holy" they were. At the same time, Jesus had kind words for a poor man who cried out in despair, "God, have mercy on me, a sinner!"

So don't worry about praying long or elaborate prayers. Just let your prayers flow from your heart. God will fill in the gaps! Here's what Jesus had to say on the subject of prayer:

"And now about prayer. When you pray, don't be like the hypocrites who love to pray publicly on street corners and in the synagogues where everyone can see them. I assure you, that is all the reward they will ever get. But when you pray, go away by yourself, shut the door behind you, and pray to your Father secretly. Then your Father, who knows all secrets, will reward you.

When you pray, don't babble on and on as people of other religions do. They think their prayers are answered only by repeating their words again and again. Don't be like them, because your Father knows exactly what you need even before you ask him!

Pray like this:

Our Father in heaven,
may your name be honored.
May your Kingdom come soon.
May your will be done here on earth,
just as it is in heaven.
Give us our food for today,
and forgive us our sins,

*just as we have forgiven those who
have sinned against us.
And don't let us yield to temptation,
but deliver us from the evil one."*

—MATTHEW 6:5-13 NLT

What a simple teaching on prayer. Find a quiet place, and talk with God like you were talking with a friend. Tell Him how you honor and thank Him. Seek His help in doing what He wants you to do. Talk about how you have wronged Him (He already knows), and ask His help in forgiving those who have wronged you. Ask Him for all you need to make it through the day. Let Him know your propensity for doing the wrong thing, and seek His help to do what is right.

Psalm 62 says, "Pour out your heart to Him." God wants us to let it all out, tell Him exactly what we are thinking and feeling. Religious prayers—those with a lot of religious cliches and phrases—are of very little value when it feels like your insides are being pulled out. You need to talk with your Father in your own words, for no one else can convey what you are feeling or going through. You will not offend God, and you cannot surprise Him! He already knows you better even than you know yourself. And He really wants to listen and help you. Prayer—the real kind that Jesus teaches—is one of the greatest privileges Jesus Freaks have.

Tell It All To God

Francois Fenelon was a seventeenth-century writer and philosopher who wrote a straightforward book about prayer called *Talking with God*. In this classic, Fenelon encourages believers to tell all to God, not just speak of "religious" things.

Talk with God with the thoughts of which your heart is full. If you enjoy the presence of God, if you feel drawn to love him, tell him so.

But what, you ask, are you to do to in times of dryness, inner resistance, and coldness? Do just the same thing. Say equally what is in your heart. Tell God that you no longer feel any love for him, that all is a terrible blank to you, that he wearies you, that his presence does not even move you, that you long to leave him for the most trifling occupation, and that you will not feel happy till you have left him and can turn to thinking about yourself. Tell him all the evil you know about yourself.

Tell Him all—the good and the bad. After all, since He can see deep into your heart, He already knows what you are thinking and how you feel. But prayer is not just about us—we are told to pray fervently for others as well.

The apostle Paul wrote to his spiritual protégé, Timothy, "I thank God, whom I serve, as my forefathers did, with a clear conscience, as night and day I constantly remember you in my prayers" (2 Timothy

1:3). Has the Holy Spirit put somebody's name or face in your thoughts? If so, stop and pray for that person, no matter where you are or what you're doing. Remember, prayer is simply talking to God in a simple, straightforward way. When you're too upset for words, it can even take the form of wordless cries coming from your spirit, but the meaning is just as real—and understandable—to the Father.

Remembering Those who Suffer

Maybe you don't know anyone who suffers for the cause of Christ, but if you've read this far you know they exist right now, all over the world. The writer of the Letter to the Hebrews tells us, "Remember those in prison as if you were their fellow prisoners, and those who are mistreated as if you yourselves were suffering" (Hebrews 13:3). Why not add these people—nameless to you but known to God—to your daily prayers? Organizations like The Voice of the Martyrs (VOM) provide followers of Jesus with Bibles, literature, and broadcasts in their native languages in restricted areas of the world where Jesus Freaks are persecuted. VOM also gives relief to the families of martyrs and helps believers rebuild their lives in countries that have suffered oppression. Their work is conducted in more than eighty nations.

Here are the links for several organizations, including VOM, that help persecuted Jesus Freaks around the world:

Jesus Freaks (www.jesusfreaks.net)

The Voice of the Martyrs (www.persecution.net)

Open Doors International (www.gospelcom.net)

Crying Voice in the Wilderness—
    Christian Martyrs (www.geocities.com/
    Athens/Ithaca/7730/Christian_martyrs/)

Religious Prisoners Congressional Task Force
    (www.house.gov/pitts)

Advocates International
    (www.advocatesinternational.org)

Freedom House Center for Religious Freedom
    (www.freedomhouse.org)

International Justice Mission (www.ijm.org)

International Missionary Center
    (www.missionary.net)

10/40 Window

In addition to suffering Jesus Freaks, people who
have yet to hear the name of Christ are in desperate
need of our prayers. Have you ever heard of the
10/40 Window? Most of the people in the world who
have never heard the gospel live in a rectangular-
shaped "window" that extends from West Africa to
East Asia, from ten degrees north to forty degrees
north of the equator. This specific region, also
known as "The Resistant Belt," is home to the major-
ity of the world's Muslims, Hindus, and Buddhists—
billions of spiritually impoverished souls.

Ministries like AD2000, Healing for the Nations,
Youth With A Mission (YWAM), and Caleb Project

raise money for and reach out to people living in the 10/40 Window. Check out the following sites and consider getting involved by supporting these ministries through your finances, your prayers, or even your time—in the form of short-term missions trips.

http://www.jesusfreaks.net
http://www.healingnations.org
http://www.ad2000.org/
http://www.ywam.org
http://www.calebproject.org

Prayer In Action

George Mueller was a troublemaker, no two ways about it. Born into a German tax collector's family, he learned to steal and gamble and drink at a young age. As a young man he often stayed in lavish hotels then sneaked out without paying his bill. He had the world in his pocket—until the day he got caught.

Jailed for his crimes, he served his term and then went right back to his reckless lifestyle. Nothing changed until a Saturday night in 1825, when he met Jesus Christ. After marrying, Mueller settled down in Bristol, England, and couldn't help but notice the many ragged children who lived on the streets. Street urchins, they were called. Most of them were either abandoned by their parents or orphaned. The Holy Spirit tugged at Mueller's heart every time he glanced at one of these children. It was time somebody did something about them.

In 1835, Mueller drew up plans for an orphanage and presented his idea at a public meeting. Money came in to support the cause. Mueller immediately rented a house and took in twenty-six children. Soon a second home was opened, then a third.

Mueller refused to ask for money from individuals or the government. Instead, he prayed. Fervently. He believed God knew about his needs at the orphanage, and he was confident that God would provide. He was right, but, as is often the case, God seemed to wait till the last moment to come through.

One morning, the breakfast table was set with plates, bowls, and cups. Only two things were missing: food and milk. The children took their places at the table and folded their hands for the blessing. Mueller led a prayer asking for their daily bread. No sooner had he finished the last word than a knock sounded at the door. It was the baker. "Mr. Mueller," he said, "I couldn't sleep last night. Somehow I felt you didn't have bread for breakfast, so I got up at 2 A.M. and baked some fresh bread." A second knock sounded. The milkman's cart had broken down right in front of the orphanage. He wondered: Could he give the children his milk so he could empty his wagon and repair it?

Over the years of his life and ministry, Mueller housed more than 100,000 orphans and recorded 50,000 answers to prayer—including millions of dollars of provisions that he prayed for. All of that without a single fund-raising campaign!

Who are some friends you are praying for? Consider keeping a journal of the prayers you pray for them and a record of God's answers to those prayers.

Who in your life is your closest confidant? How do you speak to him/her? Practice writing a prayer just as if you were talking to your trusted friend.

What percentage of your prayer time is spent with personal requests? Requests for others? How much in praise for who God is? How much in thanksgiving for all He has done? Looking at these percentages, how would you adjust your time in prayer?

The Lord's Prayer

Here's the version of the Lord's Prayer you may have memorized as a child, found in the King James Version of the Bible. But remember: What counts is not the actual words you pray but the passion behind them. Prayer is simply you talking to your Father:

> *Our Father which art in heaven,*
> *Hallowed be thy name.*
> *Thy kingdom come*
> *Thy will be done*
> *In earth, as it is in heaven.*
> *Give us this day our daily bread.*
> *And forgive us our debts*
> *As we forgive ou debtors..*
> *And lead us not into temptation,*
> *But deliver us from evil:*
> *For thine is the kingdom,*
> *And the power, and the glory,*
> *Forever. Amen.*

—MATTHEW 6:5-13 KJV

Jesus Freaks Around You Now

Strengthened by Angels
Ivan Moiseyev, 18 years old, U.S.S.R., 1970

Although he had never been there before, Private Ivan "Vanya" Moiseyev knew what awaited him at the major's office. The Communists were endlessly calling him to headquarters for talks, trying to "re-educate" him, to talk him out of his faith in God.

It was lunchtime. The sun was shining brightly in the blue sky, and the snow was glistening. As Moiseyev walked along the snowy sidewalk, he praised God for this time alone, time to sing and pray.

The morning was so bright that at first Moiseyev didn't notice; suddenly, it caught his eye. A bright star began to fall from heaven. Like a comet, it came closer and became bigger and bigger.

He looked up to see an angel above him, bright and powerful. Moiseyev's heart was filled with joy—and fear.

The angel did not descend all the way to earth, but hovered about 200 yards above the ground. He walked in the air above Moiseyev as though walking along the same road. Then the angel spoke:

"Ivan, go. Don't be afraid. I am with you."

Ivan couldn't speak, but his joy was like a fire within him. Somehow he made it to Major Gidenko's office and knocked quietly on the door.

Major Gidenko, head of the Political Directive Committee, looked up as the young soldier entered. Ivan Moiseyev had been interrogated again and again by many others and had never backed away from his faith. Still, Gidenko was certain he could solve this problem.

"Moiseyev, you don't look like a poor pupil to me. Why are you not learning the correct answers?" he asked.

"Sometimes there is a difference between the correct answers and the true ones," Ivan answered. "Sometimes God does not permit me to give 'correct' answers."

"So, God talks to you? Who is this God of yours?" As soon as he had asked the question, Gidenko regretted it. Ivan leaned forward in his chair, his face glowing with joy at the opportunity to share his faith.

"Sir, He is the One who created all the universe. He greatly loves man, and sent His Son—"

Gidenko interrupted. "Yes, yes, I know the Christian teaching. But what has that got to do with being a soldier? Do you disagree with the teaching of the glorious Red Army?"

"No, sir."

"But you do not accept the principles of scientific atheism upon which is based our entire Soviet state and the military power of the army?"

"I cannot accept what I know to be untrue. Everything else I can gladly accept."

"Moiseyev, no one can prove the existence of God. Even priests and pastors agree on that."

"Sir, they may speak about not being able to *prove* God, but there is no question about *knowing* Him. He is with me now, in this room. Before I came here, He sent an angel to encourage me."

Gidenko stared intently at Ivan. At last he spoke wearily, "I am sorry, Moiseyev, that you will not be reasonable. Your persistence will do nothing for you except bring discomfort. However, through the years I have found that men like you often come to their senses with a little discipline.

"I am ordering you to stand in the street tonight after taps are played. You will stand there until you are willing to reconsider this nonsense about talking gods and angels.

"Since the temperature is likely to be thirteen degrees below zero, for your sake, I hope you quickly agree to behave sensibly. Tomorrow we shall make a plan together for your political re-education. You are dismissed."

Gidenko expected Moiseyev to hesitate, to reconsider. Instead, he squared his shoulders and walked quietly to the door.

"Private Moiseyev!"

When the soldier turned around, Gidenko noticed he was a little pale. So Moiseyev *had* understood the order!

"You will obey my instructions in summer uniform. That is all."

That night, as the bugle sounded, Ivan made his way down the stairs of the barracks and into the snowy street. He recoiled from the icy blast of wind that burned his ears and made his eyes water. His thin summer uniform was no help in the bitter cold. He glanced at his watch. It was 10:01 P.M.

Tonight, he would have a long time to pray! But for the first time since he had been in the Soviet army, prayer did not come easily. He was worried. Could he stand out here all night? What if he froze to death? Would they let him freeze to death? What if he got so cold he gave in to their demands?

The "what ifs" flooded his mind and left it spinning. He knew he had to think of something else. Then he remembered the angel who had visited him that morning. The angel had said, "Do not be afraid, I am with you!" Suddenly he realized the angel's words had been for tonight! Although he could no longer see him, Moiseyev knew the angel was still there with him. He began to pray fervently.

At 12:30 A.M. he was distracted from his prayers by the crunching sound of footsteps in the snow. Bundled in their overcoats, hats, and boots, three officers were slowly making their way toward him.

"Private Moiseyev, have you changed your mind yet? Are you ready to come in and get warm?"

"No, comrade officers. As much as I want to come in and go to bed, I cannot. I will never agree to remain silent about God."

Even in the dim light Moiseyev could see the officers were amazed and confused. How could he stand such cold?

"Do you plan to stand out here all night long?"

"I don't see how anything else is possible, and God is helping me." Ivan checked his hands—they were cold, but not too cold. He could still move his toes easily. It was a miracle! He looked at the officers and could see that even in their coats they were already shaking from the cold. They were stamping their feet and slapping their hands, impatient to return to their heated barracks.

"You'll feel differently in another hour," the senior officer mumbled as they quickly turned away.

Ivan continued to pray for all the believers he knew. He sang Christmas carols. He prayed for every officer he knew and knew of. He cried out to God on behalf of the men in his barracks. But gradually his mind seemed to be floating somewhere outside of his head. As much as he tried, prayer eluded him.

Ivan was dozing on his feet when, at 3 A.M., the senior officer on duty woke him and let him return to the barracks.

For the next twelve nights, Ivan continued to stand in the street outside his barracks. Miraculously, he did not freeze, nor did he beg for mercy. Ivan continued to speak about his faith to his comrades and officers. He sang about the glory of Jesus Christ in his barracks, though this was strictly prohibited. To those who threatened him, he replied, "A lark threatened with death for singing would still continue to sing. She cannot renounce her nature. Neither can we Christians."

Soldiers around him were converted, impressed by his faith.

His commanders continued to interrogate him, trying to get him to deny Jesus. They put him in refrigerated cells. They clothed him in a special rubber suit, into which they pumped air until his chest was so compressed he could hardly breathe.

At the age of twenty, Ivan knew that the Communists would kill him. On July 11, 1972, he wrote to his parents, "You will not see me anymore." He then described a vision of angels and heaven that God had sent to strengthen him for the last trial.

A few days later, his body was returned to his family. It showed that he had been stabbed six times around the heart. He had wounds on his head and around the mouth. There were signs of beatings on the whole body. Then he had been drowned.

Colonel Malsin, his commander, said, "Moiseyev died with difficulty. He fought with death, but he died as a Christian."

Letter from Vanya (Ivan) to his parents—

June 15, 1972

"My dear parents, the Lord has shown the way to me . . . and I have decided to follow it. . . . I will now have more severe and bigger battles than I have had till

Faith is a lot LIKE hiking on a trail at night, GUIDED only by the beam of a flashlight.

now. But I do not fear them. He goes before me. Do not grieve for me, my dear parents. It is because I love Jesus more than myself. I listen to Him, though my body does fear somewhat or does not wish to go through everything. I do this because I do not value my life as much as I value Him. And I will not await my own will, but I will follow as the Lord leads. He says, 'Go,' and I go.

"Do not become grieved if this is your son's last letter. Because I myself, when I see and hear visions, hear how angels speak and see, I am even amazed and cannot believe that Vanya, your son, talks with angels. He, Vanya, has also had sins and failings, but through sufferings the Lord has wiped them away. And he does not live as he wishes himself, but as the Lord wishes."[7]

We continue to shout our praise even when we're hemmed in with troubles, because we know how troubles can develop passionate patience in us, and how that patience in turn forges the tempered steel of virtue, keeping us alert for whatever God will do next. In alert expectancy such as this, we're never left feeling short-changed. Quite the contrary—we can't round up enough containers to hold everything God generously pours into our lives through the Holy Spirit!

Paul the Apostle
Martyred in Rome, 65 A.D.
ROMANS 5:3-5, THE MESSAGE

Like Vanya and the apostle Paul, seek God for His direction in your life. As you press on in your faith and grow as a Jesus Freak, He will make His plan for your life clearer. But don't be surprised if He shows you just one step at a time. Faith is a lot like hiking on a trail at night, guided only by the beam of a flashlight. You have just enough light for your next step. That's God's way of stretching your faith and getting you to flex your prayer "muscles."

Jesus Freaks in the Bible

Elijah: Jesus Freak on the Run

King Ahab stroked his beard. How could he find that troublemaker Elijah? He was always one step ahead of the king's soldiers, and now he had delivered word—supposedly from God—that famine would grip the land for several years. No rain. Not even any dew, the prophet had said—until he told the sky to rain again.

Prophet! Ahab had his own prophets, 450 men who worshipped Baal. As far as he was concerned, Elijah was a dead man. A dead prophet—if only he could find him.

Far away, on a dusty road, Elijah stopped in his tracks. There was God's voice, coming to him again. "Leave here, and turn eastward. Hide in the Kerith Ravine, east of the Jordan River," the Lord instructed. "You will drink from the brook, and I have commanded the ravens to feed you."

Elijah did as the Lord told him. And, sure enough, ravens swooped down from the sky every morning and evening, bringing bread and meat. When the brook dried up, it was time to move on. Elijah always kept an eye out for his enemies; he never knew when the king's men would appear like a horde of locusts on the horizon.

Wherever God told Elijah to go, Elijah went. And wherever he went, miracles followed him. A poor widow's jar of flour and jug of oil never ran out, because she gave shelter to this prophet on the run.

When the widow's son died, Elijah raised him from the dead. But his biggest miracle was yet to come.

Elijah saw the dust cloud on the road ahead and knew someone was approaching. He recognized the man instantly—it was another prophet of the Lord. "Go tell Ahab you have found me," Elijah told the man. Obadiah was horrified. "But the king will kill me! Surely you realize he's looking for you everywhere. If I tell him you're here, and you don't show up, he'll kill me."

"As the Lord Almighty lives, whom I serve, I will surely present myself to Ahab today," Elijah replied.

He kept his word. And, with God on his side, he did even better than that. Elijah called a meeting on a mountaintop. He told Ahab to invite all the Israelites and all the prophets of Baal. It was time for a showdown.

"You wayward people," Elijah shouted. "How long will you waver between worshipping Baal and worshipping the one true God? Today I will prove to you whose God is the real one!"

Elijah commanded the prophets of Baal to build an altar. He did the same thing. Then they slaughtered two bulls and placed one on each altar. "Whoever God answers with fire is the true God!" Elijah declared. To make things more dramatic, he poured water over his altar so that the stones, the wood, and the bull were soaked. Then he asked God to show up.

"O Lord, God of Abraham, Isaac, and Israel, let it be known today that You are God in Israel and

PRAYER is power. It's supernatural FIREPOWER that wages WAR in the invisible REALM.

that I am Your servant and have done all these things at Your command. Answer me, O Lord, answer me, so these people will know that You, O Lord, are God, and that You are turning their hearts back again."

As soon as Elijah finished praying, fire crackled from heaven and burned up the sacrifice, the wood, the stones, and the soil. It also licked up the water in the trench around the altar.

When the people saw it, they fell on their faces and cried out, "The Lord—He is God! The Lord—He is God!"

Elijah turned to Ahab. "Go, eat and drink, for it's about to rain. And it's going to rain hard."

Ahab, disgusted at the prophet's arrogance, left in a huff.

As the king rode off, the sound of thunder filled the air. Black rain clouds hung low in the sky.

ChaPter THREE

Worship
like a
JESUS
Freak

Paul and Silas were in jail. Not just any jail, either. They were put into an inner cell of the prison, with their feet chained to heavy blocks of wood. This was maximum security to the max.

The situation looked hopeless. They had few friends in this city. They had no lawyer to call, no one to post bail for them. At midnight, when their situation was at its darkest, Paul and Silas used the one weapon the jailer could not take from them: worship. They started singing—loudly. Other prisoners wearing similar chains sat up in their cells and listened. Imagine that! Singing in the dungeon!

We don't know what songs these two Jesus Freaks chose. All we know is what happened as a result of Paul and Silas worshipping God. A strong earthquake rattled the prison. Doors flew open. Chains fell off. Paul and Silas were free!

Worship is a powerful instrument in the hands of a Jesus Freak. When even one person praises God, the earth shakes and prisoners are set free.

Jehoshaphat found this to be true as he faced an entire army. The combined forces of Moab and Ammon, with troops from the Meunites thrown in, were camped in En-Gedi, threatening to invade Israel. Jehoshaphat, king of Israel, sought God through prayer and fasting. The next day, he did as the Lord had instructed him to do. But the strategy was not one he had been taught in combat school.

Instead of putting his strongest, fiercest soldiers on the front line, Jehoshaphat chose to put certain men in front of the army to sing praises to God. The army of Israel advanced behind a choir! When they reached the plains where their enemies had been entrenched, instead of entering into battle, they found an abandoned field. Their enemies had fled at the mighty sound of praise. In their hurry to get away, they left behind so much bounty that it took the Israelites three days to haul it all away.

One of the Bible's most dramatic stories about the power of praise is found in the fall of Jericho. Imagine what the inhabitants of Jericho thought as they felt the huge walls of their city crumbling into the dust. And why was it falling? Not because of cannon fire. Not because of an earthquake. But because of shouts and praises to God!

Joshua had taken over command of the Israelites after Moses died. So it fell to him to take the people into the Promised Land, the place they'd been aiming for as they wandered the desert for forty years. Now their time had come. The manna no longer fell with the morning dew, because God was about to feed them from the "fat of the land" in Canaan. The only

> When **EVEN** **one** p e r s o n **PRAISES** G o d , the earth **shakes** and **prisoners** are SET **free.**

problem was that the first city they came to—
Jericho—was already occupied. And the inhabitants
of Jericho had other ideas about handing over their
city to a bunch of desert wanderers.

God had a unique plan for delivering Jericho
into the hands of His people. He told Joshua and his
fighting men to march around the city once every
day for six days, led by the priests. On the seventh
day, the people would circle the city seven times, and
on the seventh time—after the priests gave a loud
blast of their trumpets—they were to shout with all
their might to the Lord.

Not your typical battle strategy. But it worked. As
the old song says, "The walls came a-tumblin' down."
The supernatural power came not just from a physical
shout but also from the Israelites' obedience to God.
When they did what He asked them to do, no matter
how foolish they felt, the miraculous happened.

Songs of praise are a common response to
victory or hardship throughout Scripture. Moses and
his sister, Miriam, led the children of Israel in song
after they crossed the Red Sea. David wrote numerous songs to celebrate triumph over the enemy or to
plead for God's help. Solomon composed a love song
like no other to proclaim the depth of his feelings for
his beloved.

> Singing of God's awesome POWER is a FORM of spiritual warfare.

Let's be clear: Not everyone who worships God
is delivered from persecution. There are numerous
stories of followers of Jesus who have been led to
their execution while singing praise songs. But
imagine the celebration in heaven as these brothers
and sisters enter with joyful praise on their lips.

When we think of the mighty acts God has done—and will do—when songs of praise are lifted high, we no longer think of hymns as boring or choruses as repetitive. We train ourselves to recognize worship as a weapon God can use to break the chains that hold us and to free us from our prisons. Jesus Freaks sing loud!

Service as Worship

And so, dear brothers and sisters, I plead with you to give your bodies to God. Let them be a living and holy sacrifice—the kind he will accept. When you think of what he has done for you, is this too much to ask?

—ROMANS 12:1 NLT

God is honored—worshiped—when we stand before Him and say, "I am Your servant. I am willing to do whatever You would like me to do today."

Service as an act of worship can be as great as a lifetime committed to mission work or as simple as spending time with an elderly neighbor. Presenting your body (which represents your life) to God is a great act of worship.

Freak Ways to Worship

When you think of worship, you probably picture people singing in church or youth group. But as these stories about Jesus Freaks past and present have

Worship is a POWERFUL instrument in the HANDS of a Jesus Freak.

shown, you can worship God anytime, anywhere, and in just about any way you can imagine.

Don't wait until you feel like worshipping God. The Bible encourages us to praise God all the time, regardless of what's going on in our lives. In fact, when we hit the rocky times—a good friend abandons us, our parents split up, we lose our job, a loved one dies—praise and worship is transformed into a weapon, a spiritual weapon that rattles the heavens. Singing of God's awesome power is a form of spiritual warfare. God may not reverse the circumstances of your life, but you can be sure that in time He will reveal the ultimate good that came from even your darkest hours.

Here are several ways a Jesus Freak can worship outside of church:

- Sing! In the shower, standing in front of the mirror combing your hair, in the car, as you're taking a walk, doing household chores—let your imagination go wild.

- Listen to worship CDs at home, at the gym, or while shopping (using a portable CD player), or in your car.

- Play an instrument or compose a song, poem, short story, or other creative work that expresses your love for God.

- Do you lean more toward the visual arts? Create a painting or sculpture or drawing that captures what you feel deep inside when you think of what Christ did for you.

- And don't forget the performing arts. Feel free to worship God through dance, drama, mime, sign language—you complete the list!

- Journal your thoughts in an ongoing love letter to God. Journaling is a great way to have an intimate "conversation" with God. Write your thoughts, your prayers, your concerns. And leave room to record God's answers.

An Attitude of Gratitude

During one of His journeys, Jesus traveled along the border between Samaria and Galilee. As He approached a village, ten men who had leprosy met Him on the road. Aware of the law that required them to keep a distance from "clean" people, they stood a little ways off and cried out to Him, "Jesus, Master, have pity on us!"

Jesus told them to go show themselves to the priests—definitely a strange command. Only lepers who had been cleansed of their disease—and pronounced clean by the priests—could rejoin society and get a ticket out of the leper colony. But here they were, still diseased from head to toe. Or so they thought. As the men walked back to the village, they realized they had been healed.

Although ten men had been cleansed, only one, a Samaritan, turned back to thank Jesus. Luke 17:15-19 records, *One of them, when he saw he was healed, came back, praising God in a loud voice. He threw himself at Jesus' feet and thanked him. . . . Jesus asked,*

"Were not all ten cleansed? Where are the other nine? Was no one found to return and give praise to God except this foreigner?" Then he said to him, "Rise and go; your faith has made you well."

In Jesus' day, Samaritans were the outcasts of society. Yet this one outsider, a man despised by the mainstream culture, stands out in Scripture because of his thankful heart. He took the time to say "thanks" to God.

Don't allow your busy life to rob you of the blessing of a thankful heart. Become a person of gratitude. Has God blessed you with wonderful parents? Tell Him so. Did your coach believe in you when no one else on the team did? Thank him or her for it. Was your best friend there for you when your girlfriend broke up with you? Let him know how much it meant. Has God given you special talents or gifts? Remember to thank Him for it.

Jesus Freaks stand out from the crowd because they know how to thank God and others—not just sometimes, but every time!

Think of times when you felt like a "fool for Christ."
Even if people made fun of you, was it worth it?
Would you do it again?

How is praise considered to be obedience to God?

Think about the special people in your life. Have
you taken the time to thank God for them? What
else can you thank Him for?

How can you serve (present your body to God) in
your neighborhood today?

Jesus Freaks Around You Now

"If You Love Jesus, Don't Sing"
Tom White, Cuba, 1979-1980

"Well, this isn't bad," Tom White mumbled to himself. He stood in a pitch-black, cold room. He could feel the wind pouring into the room from a vent above the door. Exploring the cell, he found a bed with broken springs, a stinking mattress, and an old wooden chair nailed to the floor.

He lay down, but sleep was impossible. It was just too cold. His sleeveless coveralls were made of thin cotton, so they weren't much help. He wondered how long he could stay alive in this room.

Tom White, an American follower of Jesus, had made many successful drops of gospel literature over Cuba, distributing more than 400,000 pieces. But on May 27, 1979, his small plane crash-landed on a Cuban highway, just as he had finished a night drop. He was immediately arrested by the Communists, who questioned him and put him in solitary confinement.

Finally the guards took him to a little room for more questioning. "It sure is warm today, isn't it?" the captain taunted, taking off his military jacket to begin the interrogation. "Who do you work for?

"I work for Jesus."

"Oh, is that right? And how much money did this Jesus pay you for making these trips?"

"I took these trips for no pay. My pay is the love and blessing that God gives me for obeying Him."

Most of the captain's questions centered around money, the CIA, and revolution. These were the only concepts of power that he seemed to understand. After three or four days of cold conditions and little sleep, White was too tired to even follow his train of thought. He sat in front of his interrogator, his head drooping forward, his thoughts wandering.

How can I fight this? This could go on forever, White thought. Suddenly he had an answer. He explains:

"The Holy Spirit gave me a measure of pity and compassion for this man who was more in prison than I. I stopped responding to his questions and stared directly into his eyes. 'O God, help Captain Santos,' I prayed. 'Break through, Jesus. He is the one in the cold, for he has never felt the warmth of Your love.' I continued to pray in front of him like this for hours. His questions came less frequently until he finally stopped."

"What are you doing?" he demanded.

"I'm praying for you."

The captain's mouth dropped open. He ran one hand back through his hair, then rummaged for a cigarette. The prisoner continued to sit rigidly as he was required, looking at Santos and praying. The captain looked nervously around the room, then started drumming his fingers on the desk.

In their next session White was surprised to see him wearing sunglasses. Evidently he didn't want

White to see his eyes. *That's all right. God doesn't need eye contact. He deals with the heart,* White thought. He continued praying.

Santos sent for Major Alvarez. The major was always his last resort. Alvarez stormed into the room, red-faced and angry as usual. "So, you think this is a game?" he screamed, pounding on the desk for emphasis.

White remembers, "I was thrown into another room. Following the wall in the blackness, I discovered there was no bed or chair. The blower vent over the door was fully open. The air was pouring out at such a terrific rate that my hair was blown straight out from my head.

"I tried to walk in the pitch blackness to keep warm, holding my hands out to keep from bumping into the wall. But the wall was too cold to touch. Besides, rather than warming me, walking only brought me close to the vent. I huddled in the corner of the room.

"'O God, help me!' I cried out in despair. He would, only not in the way I wanted. I stuffed my coverall legs into my socks to keep the air from coming up my pants, then pulled my arms inside the sleeveless top. I stretched the top up over my nose so I could heat my body with my warm breath. This gave me times of relief, but then fatigue and the slow but steady loss of body heat would cause me to start shaking. I couldn't bear to sit on the floor nor lean on the wall. The only position that worked was standing, with just my forehead touching the wall.

"I don't know why I remembered to sing. But God's hand was guiding and teaching me. As the levels of punishment grew more severe, so did the intensity of spiritual warfare. Satan tried harder to drag me down, but God gently raised me up. Psalm 3:3 says, *He is my glory and the lifter of my head.* God was gracious, merciful, and loving, asking only for a chance to prove Himself to me.

"I started singing that great hymn, 'A Mighty Fortress Is Our God.' I sang 'Jesus Loves Me,' Bible choruses, and every Christian song I could remember. I was no longer conscious of the cold, only of Jesus. With eyes closed, my head barely touching the wall, I whistled, sang, even imitated a trumpet blasting out praises to the Lord.

"Although I didn't think through the many scriptures which support it, I had entered the highest level of warfare against the enemy—praise. Psalm 22:3 says that God inhabits our praises. I don't know how this is accomplished, but it's true. The mighty Deliverer, the Messiah, the Savior was with me. He held my shaking body in His arms. I was with Jesus, no matter what happened."

A guard opened the little steel window flap in the door and curiously peered inside.

"What are you doing?" he demanded.

"I'm singing about Jesus."

"Why?"

"Because I love Him," White replied happily.

He returned a few minutes later and opened the window flap again. "If you love Jesus, don't sing," he

ordered, then left. But White loved Jesus too much
to stop singing.

Over the next two days the guards came to
check on him every three or four hours. The flap
would open and a flashlight beam would snake
across the floor looking for him. Still White continued to sing. At the end of those two days, he was
returned to his former cell which, though still cold,
seemed warm in comparison. Now convinced that he
was not a super-spy trying to overthrow their
government, the authorities started White back up
the treatment ladder.

After three months, Tom White was moved from
solitary confinement to the main prison, where 7,000
prisoners were kept. There he met and worshipped
with members of the Cuban church who were
imprisoned for their faith.

An international campaign for his release helped
trim White's prison time from his original twenty-
four-year sentence. After many prayers, letters,
appeals from U.S. congressmen and even Mother
Teresa, he was released on October 27, 1980, after
seventeen months in jail. He now serves as U.S.
director for The Voice of the Martyrs.[8]

ChaPter FOUR

Study
like a
JESUS
Freak

Study. The very mention of the word is enough to ruin a good day for some people. If you're a student, you already do more cramming than you ever thought you'd do in a lifetime. So now you're expected to study the Bible too? *No thanks, man!* you may be thinking. If that sounds like you, keep reading. This chapter may challenge you and give you some surprising reasons to make studying God's Word a part of your life.

When you became a Jesus Freak you may have discovered an uncanny new attraction to the Word of God that seemed to come out of nowhere. Why? The Amplified Bible calls the Bible a "God-breathed" book (2 Timothy 3:16). That means it's way different from any other book you'll ever read. The Bible is *alive.* Once your spirit is made "alive" to Christ, it's as if you pick up the same wavelength, because the same Spirit who wrote the Bible is living in you!

Think of it like this: God put man and woman in the Garden of Eden and planned for them to enjoy a full relationship with Him. But sin entered the world when Adam and Eve fell for Satan's temptation. With that, everything changed. Death and corruption now polluted the perfect world God had created, and only one mediator could make things right again. Only Jesus Christ—the Son of God—could pay the penalty for sin and bridge the gap between God and humankind. So began a long love story where God is pictured as the pursuing "Lover" or "Bridegroom," and we humans are His "beloved" or "bride."

What does a smitten guy sometimes do for the lady of his longing? He writes her love letters— whether old-fashioned ink-on-paper, e-mails, poems, or songs. You get the picture. That formerly tough-talking guy falls head-over-heels in love, and suddenly he's writing sappy sonnets! But nobody's forcing him to. He does it because *he loves the girl and wants to win her heart.*

God wrote a series of "love letters" to us, and they're collectively called the Bible. In story after story, we see the unfolding drama of how God is calling us back to Himself. He longs to restore the relationship He intended us to have with Him. Some of the letters are in fact songs, others are genuine letters. Some are bite-sized chunks (kind of like those e-mail snippets). Still others read like biographies or long historical accounts.

When you're the object of someone's affection, it's easy to read their love letters. In fact, you're usually *eager* to do so. Try thinking that way about the Bible, and see if He doesn't surprise you with words that come to mind long after you set the Bible down!

Digging for Buried Treasure

The psalmist wrote these classic words in Psalm
119:11,16: *Your word I have hidden in my heart, that I
might not sin against You . . . I will not forget Your
word* (NKJV). Why would somebody bother to "hide"
God's Word in his heart? These verses answer that
question with at least one reason—to help you live a
pure life. But there's another reason too: You never
know when you may not have a Bible.

Someday you may have to rely on the Scriptures
stored in your heart rather than on the printed copy
of the Bible on your bookshelf. Today, while most
believers enjoy religious freedom, many Jesus Freaks
around the world are imprisoned for preaching about
Jesus Christ. They are dragged before authorities,
beaten, and even killed for having a Bible in their
possession. Imagine how precious a single copy of
the Bible would be to a Jesus Freak behind bars. For
them, the memory of verses they've read in the past
is their "Bible." It's their private buried treasure.

Persecution against the early Jesus Freaks
reached such a high pitch that martyrdom came to
be expected—even longed for by some, such as
Euplius, a man who lived in Sicily in the third
century, during the reign of Emperor Diocletian, one
of the most notorious enemies of Jesus Freaks in
history. Diocletian tried to eliminate Jesus Freaks
from the face of the earth by ordering their execution and the destruction of all their places of
worship, as well as the Bible and other writings,
Euplius was both a deacon and a Bible owner. To

> You NEVER **know when** you may not **HAVE** a **Bible.**

make sure he wasn't denied the privilege of suffering for Christ, he stood outside the Sicilian governor's office one day shouting, "I am a Christian! I desire to die for the name of Christ!"

When he was hauled before the governor, guards found a copy of the Gospels on him. "Read them," the prosecutor demanded. So Euplius began reading the words: *"Blessed are they which are persecuted for righteousness' sake: for theirs is the kingdom of heaven"* (Matthew 5:10 KJV). Then he flipped to another passage: *"Whosoever will come after me, let him take up his cross and follow me"* (Matthew 16:24 KJV).

"Why haven't you surrendered these books?" the judge interrupted.

Euplius told him that it was better to die than to give them up. "In these is eternal life," he said, "and whoever gives them up loses eternal life."

Granting his wish, the governor signaled for Euplius to be taken away. He was tortured and then executed with his Gospels tied around his neck. His last words, repeated over and over, were "Thanks be to You, O Christ. O Christ, help. It is for You that I suffer."

I am proud of the good news! It is God's powerful way of saving all people who have faith, whether they are Jews or Gentiles. The good news tells how God accepts everyone who has faith, but only those who have faith. It is just as the Scriptures say, "The people God accepts because of their faith will live."

—ROMANS 1:16-17 CEV

Putting Down Roots

Studying God's Word and reading other stories about legendary Jesus Freaks is a good way to sink deep spiritual roots in your life. Like a sturdy oak tree, a person whose roots go deep can withstand storms and dry seasons alike.

This humorous story, told in Philip Gulley's *Front Porch Tales*, illustrates that point:

I had an old neighbor when I was growing up named Doctor Gibbs. He didn't look like any doctor I'd ever known. Every time I saw him, he was wearing denim overalls and a straw hat, the front brim of which was green-sunglass plastic. He smiled a lot, a smile that matched his hat—old and crinkly and well-worn. He never yelled at us for playing in his yard. I remember him as someone who was a lot nicer than circumstances warranted.

When Doctor Gibbs wasn't saving lives, he was planting trees. His house sat on ten acres, and his life-goal was to make it a forest. The good doctor had some interesting theories concerning plant husbandry. He came from the "No pain, no gain" school of horticulture. He never watered his new trees, which flew in the face of conventional wisdom. Once I asked why. He said that watering plants spoiled them, and that if you water them, each successive tree generation will grow weaker and weaker. So you have to make things rough for them and weed out the weenie trees early on.

He talked about how watering trees made for shallow roots, and how trees that weren't watered had to grow deep roots in search of moisture. I took him to mean that deep roots were to be treasured.

So he never watered his trees. He'd plant an oak and, instead of watering it every morning, he'd beat it with a rolled up newspaper. Smack! Slap! Pow! I asked him why he did that, and he said it was to get the tree's attention.

Doctor Gibbs went to glory a couple years after I left home. Every now and again, I walk by his house and look at the trees that I'd watched him plant some twenty-five years ago. They're granite strong now. Big and robust. Those trees wake up in the morning and beat their chests and drink their coffee black.

I planted a couple trees a few years back. Carried water to them for a solid summer. Sprayed them. Prayed over them. The whole nine yards. Two years of coddling has resulted in trees that expect to be waited on hand and foot. Whenever a cold wind blows in, they tremble and chatter their branches. Sissy trees.

Funny thing about those trees of Doctor Gibbs. Adversity and deprivation seemed to benefit them in ways comfort and ease never could....

Too many times we pray for ease, but that's a prayer seldom met. What we need to do is pray for roots that reach deep into the Eternal, so when the rains fall and the winds blow, we won't be swept asunder.[9]

Let your roots grow deep. Steep yourself in the Word of God.

Bible Reading Plan

Are you ready for something really radical? With the help of the following chart, you can read the entire Word of God in a year. This schedule takes you through the Scriptures in manageable chunks, offering a different topic each day of the week.

Even if it isn't January 1, you can start today, and a year from now you will have read through the entire Bible. If you have access to a computer and want to read each day's Scripture portion online, click on this link: http://www.verseoftheday.com. The site also offers two other reading plans to choose from.

A Bible we recommend is the *Life Application Study Bible: New Living Translation* (published by Tyndale). But don't wait. Get started today with whatever Bible you have handy.

Week	The Law (Sunday)	History (Monday)	Psalms (Tuesday)	Poetry (Wednesday)	Prophecy (Thursday)	Gospels (Friday)	Epistles (Saturday)
1	Gen 1-3	Josh 1-5	Psa 1-2	Job 1-2	Isa 1-6	Matt 1-2	Rom 1-2
2	Gen 4-7	Josh 6-10	Psa 3-5	Job 3-4	Isa 7-11	Matt 3-4	Rom 3-4
3	Gen 8-11	Josh 11-15	Psa 6-8	Job 5-6	Isa 12-17	Matt 5-7	Rom 5-6
4	Gen 12-15	Josh 16-20	Psa 9-11	Job 7-8	Isa 18-22	Matt 8-10	Rom 7-8
5	Gen 16-19	Josh 21-24	Psa 12-14	Job 9-10	Isa 23-28	Matt 11-13	Rom 9-10
6	Gen 20-23	Judg 1-6	Psa 15-17	Job 11-12	Isa 29-33	Matt 14-16	Rom 11-12
7	Gen 24-27	Judg 7-11	Psa 18-20	Job 13-14	Isa 34-39	Matt 17-19	Rom 13-14
8	Gen 28-31	Judg 12-16	Psa 21-23	Job 15-16	Isa 40-44	Matt 20-22	Rom 15-16
9	Gen 32-35	Judg 17-21	Psa 24-26	Job 17-18	Isa 45-50	Matt 23-25	1 Cor 1-2
10	Gen 36-39	Ruth	Psa 27-29	Job 19-20	Isa 51-55	Matt 26-28	1 Cor 3-4
11	Gen 40-43	1 Sam 1-5	Psa 30-32	Job 21-22	Isa 56-61	Mark 1-2	1 Cor 5-6
12	Gen 44-47	1 Sam 6-10	Psa 33-35	Job 23-24	Isa 62-66	Mark 3-4	1 Cor 7-8
13	Gen 48-50	1 Sam 11-15	Psa 36-38	Job 25-26	Jer 1-6	Mark 5-6	1 Cor 9-10
14	Ex 1-4	1 Sam 16-20	Psa 39-41	Job 27-28	Jer 7-11	Mark 7-8	1 Cor 11-12
15	Ex 5-8	1 Sam 21-25	Psa 42-44	Job 29-30	Jer 12-16	Mark 9-10	1 Cor 13-14
16	Ex 9-12	1 Sam 26-31	Psa 45-47	Job 31-32	Jer 17-21	Mark 11-12	1 Cor 15-16
17	Ex 13-16	2 Sam 1-4	Psa 48-50	Job 33-34	Jer 22-26	Mark 13-14	2 Cor 1-3
18	Ex 17-20	2 Sam 5-9	Psa 51-53	Job 35-36	Jer 27-31	Mark 15-16	2 Cor 4-5
19	Ex 21-24	2 Sam 10-14	Psa 54-56	Job 37-38	Jer 32-36	Luke 1-2	2 Cor 6-8
20	Ex 25-28	2 Sam 15-19	Psa 57-59	Job 39-40	Jer 37-41	Luke 3-4	2 Cor 9-10
21	Ex 29-32	2 Sam 20-24	Psa 60-62	Job 41-42	Jer 42-46	Luke 5-6	2 Cor 11-13
22	Ex 33-36	1 Ki 1-4	Psa 63-65	Prov 1	Jer 47-52	Luke 7-8	Gal 1-3
23	Ex 37-40	1 Ki 5-9	Psa 66-68	Prov 2-3	Lamentations	Luke 9-10	Gal 4-6
24	Lev 1-3	1 Ki 10-13	Psa 69-71	Prov 4	Ezek 1-6	Luke 11-12	Eph 1-3
25	Lev 4-6	1 Ki 14-18	Psa 72-74	Prov 5-6	Ezek 7-12	Luke 13-14	Eph 4-6
26	Lev 7-9	1 Ki 19-22	Psa 75-77	Prov 7	Ezek 13-18	Luke 15-16	Phil 1-2

27	Lev 10-12	2 Ki 1-5	Psa 78-80	Prov 8-9	Ezek 19-24	Luke 17-18	Phil 3-4
28	Lev 13-15	2 Ki 6-10	Psa 81-83	Prov 10	Ezek 25-30	Luke 19-20	Col 1-2
29	Lev 16-18	2 Ki 11-15	Psa 84-86	Prov 11-12	Ezek 31-36	Luke 21-22	Col 3-4
30	Lev 19-21	2 Ki 16-20	Psa 87-89	Prov 13	Ezek 37-42	Luke 23-24	1 Thes 1-3
31	Lev 22-24	2 Ki 21-25	Psa 90-92	Prov 14-15	Ezek 43-48	John 1-2	1 Thes 4-5
32	Lev 25-27	1 Chr 1-4	Psa 93-95	Prov 16	Dan 1-6	John 3-4	2 Thes
33	Num 1-3	1 Chr 5-9	Psa 96-98	Prov 17-18	Dan 7-12	John 5-6	1 Tim 1-3
34	Num 4-6	1 Chr 10-14	Psa 99-101	Prov 19	Hosea 1-7	John 7-9	1 Tim 4-6
35	Num 7-9	1 Chr 15-19	Psa 102-104	Prov 20-21	Hosea 8-14	John 10-12	2 Tim 1-2
36	Num 10-12	1 Chr 20-24	Psa 105-107	Prov 22	Joel	John 13-15	2 Tim 3-4
37	Num 13-15	1 Chr 25-29	Psa 108-110	Prov 23-24	Amos 1-4	John 16-18	Titus
38	Num 16-18	2 Chr 1-5	Psa 111-113	Prov 25	Amos 5-9	John 19-21	Philemon
39	Num 19-21	2 Chr 6-10	Psa 114-116	Prov 26-27	Obadiah	Acts 1-2	Heb 1-4
40	Num 22-24	2 Chr 11-15	Psa 117-118	Prov 28	Jonah	Acts 3-4	Heb 5-7
41	Num 25-27	2 Chr 16-20	Psa 119	Prov 29-30	Micah	Acts 5-6	Heb 8-10
42	Num 28-30	2 Chr 21-24	Psa 120-121	Prov 31	Nahum	Acts 7-8	Heb 11-13
43	Num 31-33	2 Chr 25-28	Psa 122-124	Eccl 1-2	Habakkuk	Acts 9-10	James 1-3
44	Num 34-36	2 Chr 29-32	Psa 125-127	Eccl 3-4	Zephaniah	Acts 11-12	James 4-5
45	Deut 1-3	2 Chr 33-36	Psa 128-130	Eccl 5-6	Haggai	Acts 13-14	1 Pet 1-3
46	Deut 4-6	Ezra 1-5	Psa 131-133	Eccl 7-8	Zechariah 1-7	Acts 15-16	1 Pet 4-5
47	Deut 7-9	Ezra 6-10	Psa 134-136	Eccl 9-10	Zechariah 8-14	Acts 17-18	1 John 1-2
48	Deut 10-12	Neh 1-4	Psa 137-139	Eccl 11-12	Malachi	Acts 19-20	1 John 3-4
49	Deut 13-15	Neh 5-9	Psa 140-142	Song 1-2	Rev 1-6	Acts 21-22	1 John 5
50	Deut 16-18	Neh 10-13	Psa 143-145	Song 3-4	Rev 7-11	Acts 23-24	2 John
51	Deut 19-21	Esther 1-5	Psa 146-148	Song 5-6	Rev 12-17	Acts 25-26	3 John
52	Deut 22-24	Esther 6-10	Psa 149-150	Song 7-8	Rev 18-22	Acts 27-28	Jude

A Taste for the Classics

To further ground you in the faith, round out your Bible reading with biographies of great men and women of God. Or choose one or two spiritual classics, and make it a priority to read them in the next few months. Here's a list to get you started:

- *With Christ in the School of Prayer* by Andrew Murray
- *The Practice of the Presence of God* by Brother Lawrence
- *My Utmost for His Highest* by Oswald Chambers
- *The Screwtape Letters* by C.S. Lewis
- *Mere Christianity* by C.S. Lewis (actually, anything by C.S. Lewis)
- *The Cost of Discipleship* by Dietrich Bonhoeffer
- *The Confessions* by St. Augustine
- *Spiritual Classics: Selected Readings for Individuals and Groups on the Twelve Spiritual Disciplines* by Richard J. Foster and Emilie Griffin, editors
- *The Pilgrim's Progress* by John Bunyan
- *A Shepherd Looks at the Twenty-Third Psalm* by Phillip Keller
- *Imitation of Christ* by Thomas à Kempis
- *Dark Night of the Soul* by St. John of the Cross

- *The Mark of the Christian, The God Who Is There*, and others by Francis A. Schaeffer

Your life as a Jesus Freak will take on a new dimension as you soak your mind in God's Word and the words of other Jesus Freaks. Take your study time seriously—the reward will show up in the way your spirit grows strong. The roots you water today will grow deep over time, and you'll find yourself like Doctor Gibbs' oak trees—able to withstand any storm that attempts to topple you.

"When you were a child, you might have sat on a small stool and looked at your mother's embroidery. From your point of view, it was a confusion of zigzags, knots, and loose threads. Then your mother, to help you understand, turned the embroidery on the right side so you could see and appreciate the design.

"You must stop looking on the wrong side of things. . . . Lift your hearts to heavenly places and look down upon events from that vantage point. You will see life's temporary sufferings as a gathering of pearls and jewels with which we will be adorned in eternity."

Richard Wurmbrand
Imprisoned for a total of fourteen years
Romania
1940s, '50s, and '60s

The
BIBLE
is
alive.

Jesus Freaks Around You

Reading the Walls
Korea, 1866

When he heard the shouts, Robert J. Thomas looked up from reading his Bible. Korean soldiers were boarding the ship, waving long knives that flashed in the light. When he saw that he was going to be killed, he held out the Korean Bible to them saying, "Jesus, Jesus." His head was cut off.

Robert J. Thomas, the first missionary to Korea, survived only a few months in that country. He had been ordained on June 4, 1863, at a little church in Hanover, Wales. He and his wife left for Korea in July, sent by the London Mission Society. His wife died soon after arriving at Shanghai, China.

Thomas went on alone to Korea, where he began to learn the language and evangelize. In 1866, Thomas rode the American ship, *The General Sherman,* along the Taedong River (where the capital of North Korea is today). When the *Sherman* ran aground on a sandbar, the Korean soldiers on shore became suspicious, boarded the ship, and killed the foreigners, including Thomas.

Twenty-five years after Thomas' death, someone discovered a little guesthouse in the area where he had lived. Its wallpaper bore Korean characters. The owner of the house explained that he had pasted the pages of a book on the wall to preserve the writing. Not only the owner but also many of the guests

would come in and stay for hours to read the walls—
to read the pages of the Bible Thomas had given to
his murderers.

Even though North Korea is now ruled by
Communists, the church lives. The work of Robert
J. Thomas, the short-lived missionary, continues.
Today, more than 100 families secretly worship Jesus
Christ in this area. God's Word has gone from being
hidden inside their walls to being hidden inside
their hearts.

Many would call Thomas' years of preparation a
waste. He worked so long for only three brief
months in which he did not lead even one person to
Jesus, and it cost him and his wife their lives. But
God can always take what seems like failure and
turn it into success. Though Thomas died before
leading anyone to Christ, he penetrated the darkness
of that land with the Word of God. The Word
Thomas deposited there created a pocket of light that
still perseveres today.

Jesus Freaks in the Bible

Elisha: A Double Portion

Ever since the day Elijah threw his cloak over Elisha, things had not been the same. The elder prophet spotted Elisha plowing in his father's fields. The young man ran up to Elijah.

"Wait! Just let me say good-bye to my mother and father, and I will come with you," he said between breaths. Elijah took off his cloak and placed it on the young man's shoulders.

And so began one of the greatest power duos recorded in the Bible. Elijah was a man both feared and hated—feared because he spoke for the one true God, not the false gods the Israelites had started to worship. Hated, because he stirred up trouble for the king and queen, Ahab and Jezebel. Never had a more evil pair sat on the throne of Israel, and Elijah let them know it.

Now he trained Elisha to follow in God's ways too. When the time came for Elijah to leave the earth, he told Elisha he would see him no more. "Tell me, what can I do for you before I am taken from you?" he asked.

Elisha thought for a minute. Boldness surged through his veins. "Let me inherit a double portion of your spirit!" he blurted.

"You have asked a difficult thing," the old prophet answered. "Yet, if you see me when I am taken from you, it will be yours—otherwise not."

As they walked along, suddenly a chariot blazing with fire appeared in the sky. In a flash Elijah was gone, carried away on a whirlwind. Elisha stared, his mouth open. God had granted his request.

The miracles Elisha performed outstripped even the amazing feats done by his mentor. Elisha caused water to flow into a valley filled with ditches; he turned poisoned food into a harmless bowl of soup; he miraculously purified the water in a contaminated well; he raised a dead boy to life again; he fed 100 hungry men from twenty loaves of barley bread; he made the head of an axe float on water; and he enlisted an army of angels to wage war against an enemy nation.

Because Elisha was faithful to follow God's orders and speak His word to the people, God gave him a supernatural power that continues to amaze Jesus Freaks to this day.

ChaPter FIVE

Love
like a
JESUS
Freak

Cross-Cultural Love

Love—true love—celebrates all colors. Racial prejudice is still very much a problem throughout the world. The Good News is that Jesus' love is strong enough to break down the walls that separate the races. As Michael Tait sings in "American Tragedy,"

> *Love's our common ground*
> *Yeah, my skin is brown*
> *Ain't no sweeter sound*
> *Walls are tumblin' down*

But there are other cultural prejudices that keep us from embracing others with the love of God.

Perhaps you have problems reaching out to those in your city who live in poverty. They dress poorly, they drive rusty "beater" cars, and they live in run-down houses or apartments. Yet Jesus calls us to *love* them.

Maybe your cultural barrier is age. After all, what do you have in common with people twice, even three times your age? How can you even like them when they are constantly complaining about how you dress and the music you play? Yet Jesus calls us to love them.

If you struggled to get through high school, do you have trouble carrying on a conversation with a college graduate? That may be your cultural barrier. Do you stay away from people who are physically or mentally challenged? That is a cultural prejudice. Jesus calls us to love other people the way He loves us.

Imagine the unimaginable for a moment. Imagine a *sculptor* becoming a *sculpture*. Impossible, you say? In that same way, God the Creator became one of His creations by being born a baby among us. That is a cultural gap too wide to even begin to understand. If Jesus can do *that* for us, He can help us take His love across our prejudices.

In her book *Out of the Saltshaker & Into the World,* Rebecca Pippert tells the story of how one man crossed a cultural gap in a profound way:

When I first came to Portland, Oregon, I met a student on one of the campuses where I worked. He was brilliant and looked like he was always pondering the esoteric. His hair was always messy, and in the entire time I know him, I never once saw him

wear a pair of shoes. Rain, sleet, or snow, Bill was
always barefoot.

While he was attending college, he had become a
Christian. At this time, a well-dressed, middle-class
church across the street from the campus wanted to
develop more of a ministry to the students. The
congregation was not sure how to go about it, but
they tried to make the students feel welcome. One
day, Bill decided to worship there. He walked into
this church, wearing his blue jeans, T-shirt, and, of
course, no shoes. People looked a bit uncomfortable,
but not one said anything to him. Bill began walking
down the aisle looking for a seat. The church was
quite crowded that Sunday, so as he got down to the
front pew and realized that there were no seats, he
just squatted on the carpet—perfectly acceptable
behavior at the college fellowship, but perhaps
unnerving for a church congregation. The tension in
the air became so thick one could slice it.

Just then, an elderly man began walking down the
aisle toward the boy. Was he going to scold Bill? My
friends who saw him approaching thought, "You
can't blame him. He'd never guess Bill is a Christian.
And his world is too distant from Bill's to understand.
You can't blame him for what he's going to do."

As the man kept walking slowly down the aisle, the
church became utterly silent. All eyes were focused
on him; you could not hear anyone breathe. The
man reached Bill, and with some difficulty he
lowered himself and sat down next to him on the
carpet. He and Bill worshipped together on the floor

that Sunday. I was told there was not a dry eye in the house.[10]

That is cross-cultural love, the willingness to come out of your comfort zone and worship with others in theirs. It takes guts, but that is love in action.

When we stop to think of the person we are talking with or ministering to as an individual—not as part of a specific cultural group but as a person God created and Jesus died for—it helps make the barriers disappear.

One man who knew what it means to be a Jesus Freak across cultural barriers was the man called America's Bishop—the late Fulton Sheen. The story is told of Bishop Sheen's visit to a leper colony in Africa. He brought with him 500 shiny silver crosses to give to those at the colony.

The first man to approach Bishop Sheen had no left arm. His right arm and hand were disfigured, covered with the white, open sores of the hideous skin disease. The leper held out his rotting hand and looked into the eyes of Bishop Sheen. Sheen held the cross a few inches above the man's hand and dropped it into his palm.

"At that moment," recalled Sheen many years later, "there were 501 lepers in that camp, and the most leprous of all was myself. I had taken the symbol of redemption, of Divine Love for man, of the humiliation of Divinity, and had refused to identify myself with all that that symbol implied."

Sheen realized that while he had come to share the love of Jesus with a whole colony of lepers, once

The Good News is that Jesus' LOVE is strong enough to BREAK down the walls that separate the RACES.

he met a particular leper, it took a special effort to show that love.

"I looked at the crucifix in the putrid mass of his hand," said Sheen, "and realized that I, too, must become one with suffering humanity."

Bishop Sheen pressed his hand to the hand of the leper, and continued to do that for the other 499 lepers. That is love across barriers.[11]

Pray that God helps you break down cultural prejudices and barriers that are keeping you from carrying His love to hurting, needy people.

Radical Love on the Battlefield

Have you ever been away from home and yearned for something to eat or drink that was only available in your hometown? Perhaps a slice of your favorite pizza or a scoop of that famous frozen custard?

King David was on the battlefield, far from his home in Bethlehem, and he had a craving. All he wanted was a glass of water. Let's look at how love in action helped to quench David's thirst.

One year at harvest time, the Three Warriors went to meet David at Adullam Cave. The Philistine army had set up camp in Rephaim Valley and had taken over Bethlehem. David was in his fortress, and he was very thirsty. He said, "I wish I had a drink from the well by the gate at Bethlehem."

*The Three Warriors sneaked into the Philistine camp
and got some water from the well near Bethlehem's gate.
But after they brought the water back to David, he
refused to drink it. Instead, he poured it out as a sacrifice and said to the LORD, "I can't drink this water! It's
like the blood of these men who risked their lives to get
it for me"*

—2 SAMUEL 23:13-17 CEV

Is there someone you love enough to risk your
life for in order to satisfy a want or a need in their
life? Do you have a friend who will risk all for you?

Loving Your Enemies

Jerusalem is a hot, dusty place. Beads of sweat
broke out on Stephen's face as he told the small
crowd gathered how belief in Jesus of Nazareth had
changed his life. Some sneered and walked away;
others came a little closer, their hearts and ears drawn
by the strange words of this ordinary-looking man.

When word reached the synagogue that Stephen
was stirring up crowds—and also performing miracles—the religious leaders accused him of blasphemy
and hauled him before the Sanhedrin. *Let him defend
himself before the council,* they thought smugly. *We'll
see how far his fantasy stories get him.*

The council members got more than they
bargained for. This radical Jesus Freak opened his
mouth and delivered one of the longest speeches
recorded in the New Testament. He told them how

God had pursued them like a divine Lover, yet they had killed His messengers and finally even murdered His Son.

"You stiff-necked people," Stephen shouted. "You are just like your fathers: You always resist the Holy Spirit!"

That did it. The religious leaders grabbed Stephen by his neck and dragged him outside the city walls to a rocky place. Convinced they were carrying out justice, they heaved large stones out of the ground and hurled them at Stephen. A heavy rock hit him on the head, then another. As the crowd grew bloodthirsty, the stones rained down on him.

Stephen, crumpled on the ground, lifted his eyes toward heaven. "Lord Jesus, receive my spirit." Then, crawling to his knees, he cried out, "Lord, do not hold this sin against them." They were the last words he would utter.

Loving your enemies is one of the surest signs of a Jesus Freak. Only the love of God inside a human heart can produce such astonishing results. From the cradle on up we are conditioned to love those who love us, to defend ourselves against bullies and to give "an eye for an eye" when things turn ugly. But once God turns our spirit inside out, He changes our vengeful attitude to "Father, forgive them. They don't know what they do."

Remember the story of Maria and Varia in *Jesus Freaks?* Imprisoned in Communist U.S.S.R., Varia was thin, pale, and beaten, but her eyes shone with the peace of God as she told Maria she was happy to "endure for His name." The two Russian teenagers

LOVING your enemies is one of the SUREST signs of a Jesus Freak.

had once been schoolmates in a Communist boarding school. Varia, a member of the Communist Youth Organization, had constantly teased Maria, a Jesus-follower. In response, Maria prayed for her friend with special concern.

One day Varia said, "I cannot understand what a being you are. Here so many insult and hurt you, and yet you love everyone."

"God has taught us to love everyone, not only friends but also enemies," Maria answered.

"Can you love me too?" Varia asked, and the two friends wept and hugged. Not long afterward Varia became a Jesus Freak and witnessed openly to everyone about it—even at the Communist Youth Club meeting. Her bold stand for Christ earned her a stay in prison, where the two friends had a brief meeting before Varia was shipped to a Siberian labor camp. Months of silence followed. Finally, Maria received a letter. In it Varia wrote:

My heart praises and thanks God that, through you, He showed me the way to salvation…Who can separate us from the love of God in Christ? Nobody and nothing. Neither prison nor suffering. The sufferings that God sends us only strengthen us more and more in the faith of Him. My heart is so full that the grace of God overflows. At work they curse and punish me, giving me extra work because I cannot be silent. I must tell everyone what the Lord has done for me.

Loving those who hate us may result in bruised bodies or bruised spirits, yet Jesus promised that this trait would distinguish true believers from those who merely give it lip service. We can't muster up the power to love the unlovable any more than we can grit our teeth and stop feeling pain when a pounding hammer meets our thumb. But the supernatural presence of God in us does something that proves again and again the truth of this statement: When God "owns" us, we are never the same again.

Let the God-kind of love be your trademark. At school, at work, at church, at the mall, in your neighborhood, on the basketball court—wherever you find yourself, allow the Holy Spirit to speak through you. Let Him guide your actions. The change in you may astonish others at first (including yourself), but keep at it. Love like that is love worth giving throughout a lifetime.

Let's be clear: None of us can muster up the deep love of God on our own. We can only love each other because Christ first loved us. He showed this by freely laying down His life for us. We did nothing to earn this love, but still He generously gives it to us. He frees us to receive His love and to give love to others.

To see more of the depth of God's love, spend time with 1 Corinthians chapter 13 and John chapter 15.

What barriers surround your heart? Which cultural groups or races do you struggle to associate with?

Who are the lepers of our society today? How can we press our hand into theirs?

How would you react if someone out of the ordinary began to attend your church and worship in a different way?

How can you show radical love—even to those you don't like?

Action Points

Do you want to love like a Jesus Freak? Try these ideas on for size:

- [Guys] Invite the local outcast to play a game of pickup basketball with you. If he's uncomfortable playing sports, offer to just hang out with him. Treat him as you would your best friend.

- [Girls] Ask that "unpopular" girl in your neighborhood or school to go see a movie with you. Or go on a shopping spree together. You may be surprised at the person you find lurking beneath that "uncool" exterior.

- Offer to clean the house for a neighbor or a relative—no strings attached.

- Spend a whole afternoon with your little brother or sister doing what they think is fun.

- Go out of your way to talk kindly to one elderly person this week. Our society often treats them like throwaways. Show them the love of Christ, and try to see past their wrinkles to the young man or woman they once were—someone not so different from you, really.

ChaPter SIX

Stand
like a
JESUS
Freak

Taking a stand makes you stand out. Think about it. It's much easier to go with the flow, to follow the crowd and blend in. Dress the same. Talk the same. Live the same. Wear your hair the same way. Tune in the same music. Follow the code.

No wonder so many people do just that. It makes life simpler and keeps rejection at arm's length. So what do you do when you become a Jesus Freak? Suddenly you find yourself going against the flow. This river you've been riding is rushing downstream, and now you're paddling upstream against a stiff current. Maybe you've been caught in the rapids a few times. Maybe the whitewater has threatened to pull you back into the current—back where you used to be, back where life was easy but empty.

So what do you do? You find a Rock to climb up on, and there you stand. Jesus told a story once about anchoring your life on a Rock. Here's what He said:

"So why do you call me 'Lord,' when you won't obey me? I will show you what it's like when someone comes to me, listens to my teaching, and then obeys me. It is like a person who builds a house on a strong foundation laid upon underlying rock. When the floodwaters rise and break against the house, it stands firm because it is well built. But anyone who listens and doesn't obey is like a person who builds a house without a foundation. When the floods sweep down against that house, it will crumble into a heap of ruins."

—LUKE 6:46-49 NLT

The apostle Paul wrote:

For no one can lay any other foundation than the one we already have—Jesus Christ. Now anyone who builds on that foundation may use gold, silver, jewels, wood, hay, or straw. But there is going to come a time of testing at the judgement day to see what kind of work each builder has done. Everyone's work will be put through the fire to see whether or not it keeps its value. If the work survives the fire, that builder will receive a reward. But if the work is burned up, the builder will suffer great loss. The builders themselves will be saved, but like someone escaping through a wall of flames.

—1 CORINTHIANS 3:11-15 NLT

If you are a Jesus Freak, you're already starting to build your "house" on the Rock. Every time you hang out with other believers, every time you read the Bible, every time you pray, every time you encourage a fellow Jesus Freak, every time you stand up for what's right . . . you're adding another brick to your foundation. Don't let anything keep you from building a house that can stand strong—battered but not broken, weathered but wiser. Because the wisdom you acquire that way will surely be the Godly kind.

"Blessed Are Those Who Are Persecuted . . ."

"John Hus!"

The cry broke the silence of the dark cell where Hus spent his days and nights in an agonizing sameness. The door creaked open, and Hus blinked as his eyes focused on the four bishops who stood before him. He knew what they wanted: They had come to find out if he would continue his stand—or back down.

A fifth person stood with the bishops. It was Hus' friend, Lord John de Clum. "Master John Hus," he pleaded, "I encourage you: If you know you are guilty of any of the charges brought against you, don't be ashamed to admit you were wrong and change your mind."

De Clum paused and glanced down for a second. Then his eyes met Hus' with a steady gaze. "On the other hand, please don't betray your own conscience. It is better to suffer any punishment than deny what you have known to be the truth."

With tears in his eyes, John Hus answered his friend: "As the Most High God is my witness, I am ready with my heart and mind to change my stand if the council can teach me by the holy Scripture and convict me of error."

The bishops shook their heads and murmured among themselves, "See how stubborn he is? He is so full of pride, he prefers his own thinking over the opinions of the whole council."

Disgusted, they commanded the guards to return Hus to his cell. The next day he would be sentenced to death.

John Hus was a priest during the 1400s in what is now Czechoslovakia. He spoke out for religious freedom and the right of an individual to have a personal relationship with God—not just a relationship with the church, which was controlled by the priests. He boldly confronted church leaders who were not living Christlike lives. He also protested the death sentence for those who didn't agree with the teaching of the church.

Expelled from the church for his radical beliefs, Hus nonetheless continued to preach and won the hearts of common people and nobles alike. Summoned to appear before the church council in 1413, Hus went willingly, thankful for the chance to explain his beliefs. But he walked right into a trap.

Before he could say a word, the church leaders had him thrown into prison. After nineteen months he was finally put on trial. At the trial, every time Hus opened his mouth to speak, the noise of the crowd drowned out his defense. So the council simply read the charges against him and then read portions of his books as his answers.

They told him, "If you will humbly confess that you have been wrong, promise never to teach these things again, and publicly take back all you have said, we will have mercy on you and restore your honor."

"I am in the sight of the Lord my God," Hus replied through tears. "I can by no means do what you want me to do. How could I face God? How could I face the great number of people I have taught? They now have the most firm and certain knowledge of the Scriptures and are armed against all the assaults of Satan. How can I, by my example, make them uncertain? I cannot value my own body more than their health and salvation!"

The council dressed Hus in priestly robes and ornaments, then one by one removed them in a symbolic gesture of stripping him of his priestly privileges. Finally, the only thing remaining that identified him as a priest was his hair, which was shaved bald on top. In the end they removed this too, cutting off the skin on the top of his head with a pair of scissors. The council condemned him to death by fire.

As guards led John Hus outside the gates, the whole city followed after him. When he reached the place of execution, he knelt and prayed Psalm 31 and Psalm 51, and then said, "Into Thy hands, O Lord, I commit my spirit: Thou has redeemed me, O most good and merciful God!"

Pulling him up from his prayers, the hangman tied him to the stake with wet ropes. His neck was tied to the stake with a chain. Seeing it, John smiled and told his executioners, "My Lord Jesus Christ was bound with a harder chain than this for my sake, and why then should I be ashamed of this rusty one?"

Bundles of sticks, piled chin high, were placed around Hus.

Given one last chance to renounce his beliefs, Hus replied: "What error should I renounce? I am guilty of no wrong. I taught all men repentance and remission of sins, according to the truth of the gospel of Jesus Christ. For that gospel I am here, with a cheerful mind and courage, ready to suffer death. What I taught with my lips I now seal with my blood."

As the fire was lit, John Hus started singing a hymn with such a loud voice that he could be heard over the crackling fire and the heckling of the crowd. His song: "Jesus Christ! The Son of the living God! Have mercy on me."[12]

What's Right Is Right

Escorted to Rome by burly Roman guards, the apostle Paul stood alone before the emperor, the most powerful man of his day. Later, he wrote these words to his spiritual son, Timothy: *When I was first put on trial, no one helped me . . . But the Lord stood beside me. He gave me . . . strength* (2 Timothy 4:16-17 CEV).

Another man, centuries later, stood before the highest ruler on earth. Like Paul, he was there to defend his belief that Jesus, and the Scriptures, were intended for everyone. And, also like Paul, he found that God provides supernatural courage when you need it most.

Martin Luther taught that everyone, not just priests, should be allowed to read the Bible. When Pope Leo demanded that Luther stop teaching this, Luther burned the pope's orders. His action so enraged the pope that a meeting was arranged to hash out all the problems.

Pope Leo lined up lawyers to attend the meeting, hoping to discredit Luther. Meanwhile, Luther planned to defend himself, even at the risk of his life. "I will not flee, still less recant," Luther said as he prepared for the journey. "May the Lord Jesus strengthen me." And so he set out from his home in Wittenberg, Germany, for the ten-day trip to Worms, where the meeting would be held. As Luther rode along in a cart, crowds gathered along the road. Bold as ever, he preached to them.

But Luther's three traveling companions grew worried as they drew near to Worms. "What if you end up like John Hus?" they said.

"Though Hus was burned," Luther said, "the truth was not burned, and Christ still lives . . . I shall go to Worms, though there were as many devils there as tiles on the roofs."

He arrived in Worms to the sound of horns blowing. The city watchmen alerted everyone that the heretic Martin Luther was approaching. Stepping from his wagon, Luther whispered, "God will be with me!"

God PROVIDES supernatural courage when you NEED it the most.

Standing up for **what's** RIGHT always GOES against the current, but it's the ONLY way to be HEADING if you're a Jesus Freak.

As he stood before Emperor Charles V and the Imperial Congress, Luther must have felt overwhelmed. History records that he mumbled and almost collapsed. But the next day, buoyed by prayer, he shouted out, "I cannot and will not recant! Here I stand. God help me! Amen."

Luther's bold words caused a near riot, and the congress was adjourned.

Later, Luther said, "I was fearless. I was afraid of nothing; God can make one so desperately bold."

That boldness continued, and no doubt it fueled the action for which history most remembers this Jesus Freak. Fed up with the church's false teachings, Martin Luther nailed a scathing document to the door of the church in Wittenberg. In that one gesture, he started the Reformation and paved the way for modern-day Jesus Freaks to read the Bible for themselves and not just be spoon-fed whatever the wayward priests wanted them to know.

Standing up for what's right always goes against the current, but it's the only way to be heading if you're a Jesus Freak.

Keeping Pure in a Perverse World

Sex. It drives our culture. It shouts to us from billboards, magazine covers, music videos, movies, the Internet—and from our peers. Taking a stand for purity is one of the most difficult things you'll ever do as a Jesus Freak. Earlier generations expected young men and women (especially) to save sex for marriage. Today, virgins often feel like geeks and social outcasts. Some people even concoct lies about sexual conquests that never happened, just so they can feel as if they fit in with those more sexually experienced.

So why does God have to be so demanding, anyway? Why does He give us hormones, then drive us crazy with "No Trespassing!" rules? The answer is found in 1 Corinthians 6.

The apostle Paul had a tough case on his hands. He had to mentor the new Jesus Freaks in Corinth, a city known for its perverse, sensual culture. This new band of believers struggled with their sex drives after they came to Christ, and Paul wrote them a letter that went like this:

> *You know the old saying, "First you eat to live, and then you live to eat"? Well, it may be true that the body is only a temporary thing, but that's no excuse for stuffing your body with food, or indulging it with sex. Since the Master [Jesus] honors you with a body, honor him with your body!*
>
> *God honored the Master's body by raising it from the grave. He'll treat yours with the same resurrection power. Until that time, remember that your bodies are created with the same dignity as the Master's body. You wouldn't take the Master's body off to a whorehouse, would you? I should hope not.*

There's more to sex than mere skin on skin. Sex is as much spiritual mystery as physical fact. As written in the Scripture, "The two become one." Since we want to become spiritually one with the Master, we must not pursue the kind of sex that avoids commitment [marriage] and intimacy, leaving us more lonely than ever—the kind of sex that can never "become one." There is a sense in which sexual sins are different from all others. In sexual sin we violate the sacredness of our own bodies, these bodies that were made for God-given and God-modeled love, for "becoming one" with another. Or didn't you realize that your body is a sacred place, the place of the Holy Spirit? Don't you see that you can't live however you please, squandering what God paid such a high price for? The physical part of you is not some piece of property belonging to the spiritual part of you. God owns the whole works. So let people see God in and through your body.

—1 Corinthians 6:13-20, The Message

In the next portion of his letter, Paul writes, *Sexual drives are strong, but marriage is strong enough to contain them and provide for a balanced and fulfilling sexual life in a world of sexual disorder* (1 Corinthians 7:3-4 The Message).

You may be thinking, "But I'm too young to get married." (You're probably right!) "What do I do till then?"

The answer is found in one word: wait. This is easy to say, and often very hard to accomplish. Paul said he trained his body into submission, the way an athlete undergoes rigorous training for a competition. The training may be hard work and not gratifying to the body, but the rewards of winning will be worth the effort.

What if it's too late to save your purity? What if you already blew it? First of all, take heart. God's grace runs so far and wide and deep that you can never escape it. His Spirit within will prompt you to get up when you fall. He will prod you on, encouraging you to make a new start. If you feel able to, share your struggles with one or two trusted friends. (Note: These must be trustworthy individuals of proven character!) Commit to help keep each other accountable. Pray for each other. Take part in group activities, and avoid situations that have the potential for disaster, such as being alone with someone you're attracted to.

With practice, saying no to sensuality becomes like any other learned behavior—it forms into a habit. And a life of purity is not only a gift to God and yourself, it's a gift to your future spouse.

Having Done All, Stand

Taking a stand doesn't always lead to life-threatening declarations, though for some it may. Remember the Columbine High School shootings? Cassie Bernall was killed because she stood firm in

God's **GRACE** runs so **far** and **deep** and **wide** that you can **NEVER** escape it.

her declaration for God. But for most of us, taking a stand means staying alert to seemingly little things that can trip us. How can you make a stand as a Jesus Freak when . . .

- You're at a party, and a few so-called friends pressure you to bend your rules "just this once" and take drugs?

- You see a group of cool kids making fun of that quiet girl who always totes around her Bible?

- A friend is waiting for you at the theater, waving you inside past the ticket counter. You could probably slip inside without being seen.

- You're hanging with the guys, and a pretty girl walks by. The others start whistling and making lewd remarks. What do you do?

- A customer at the store where you work overpays you by a dollar, and you are tempted to pocket the "extra" money rather than give it back.

We are Christ's ambassadors, and God is using us to speak to you. We urge you, as though Christ himself were here pleading with you, "Be reconciled to God!"

Paul the Apostle
Martyred in Rome, 65 A.D.

2 CORINTHIANS 5:20 NLT

How can you hold your ground when all around you is shaking?

Have you "built" your life on the words of Jesus—or on the words of the world?

Jesus Freaks Around You Now

'I am the Way, the Truth, and the Life'
Zahid, Pakistan, around 1986

"When you catch the infidels, beat them! Allah will be pleased," Zahid shouted. The crowd of young men, the youth group of his mosque, waved their sticks and iron bars and cheered in agreement. Zahid's arrogance and hatred swelled. He felt he was doing well as a young Muslim priest. His parents would be proud. He had rallied a rather large group for this outing, and they were nearly ready to go. Within minutes they would be combing the streets of their village looking for Jesus Freaks to ambush.

Zahid had a proud heritage in Pakistan. His father and older brother were Muslim priests. As expected, Zahid had followed in their footsteps. Shortly after he was assigned to his first mosque, his hatred for Jesus-followers began to show as he rallied his followers against them.

To Zahid, as to many Muslims, those who follow Jesus are heretics and should be punished. His government is becoming increasingly influenced by *Sharia* law in some provinces. *Sharia* law calls for the death of anyone found guilty of blasphemy against the prophet Mohammed or the Koran. To these Muslims, rejecting Mohammed's teachings by becoming a Jesus Freak is the highest form of blasphemy.

When their passion peaked, Zahid led his group into the streets. Soon they found a group of young Jesus-followers to attack. As the mob descended on

them, the young boys ran, one of them dropping his
Bible. One of Zahid's group stopped, picked up the
Bible, and opened it to rip out its pages. Zahid had
always told his followers to burn all the Bibles they
collected, but this time Zahid felt strangely
compelled to keep it and study it in order to expose
its errors to the people of his mosque. He quickly
snatched the book from the man, encouraged him to
chase the fleeing Jesus Freaks, and tucked the Bible
into his shirt to look at later.

Zahid reported in his own words what became
of keeping that Bible:

"I was reading the Bible, looking for contradic-
tions I could use against the Christian faith. All of a
sudden, a great light appeared in my room and I
heard a voice call my name. The light was so bright,
it lit the entire room.

"Then the voice asked, 'Zahid, why do you
persecute Me?'

"I was scared. I didn't know what to do. I
thought I was dreaming. I asked, 'Who are you?'

"I heard, 'I am the way, the truth, and the life.'

"For the next three nights the light and the
voice returned. Finally, on the fourth night, I knelt
down, and I accepted Jesus as my Savior."

Zahid's hatred was suddenly gone. All he wanted
to do was share Jesus with everyone he knew. He
went to his family members and those in the mosque
and told them what had happened to him over the
previous four nights, but they didn't believe him. His
family and friends turned against him. They called

the authorities to have him arrested so he would leave them alone about this Jesus. According to Islamic teaching, Zahid was now considered an apostate: a traitor to Islam, a man who had turned from his faith and accepted stupid lies. Thus, he was a criminal.

Zahid was locked up in prison for two years. The guards repeatedly beat and tortured him. One time, they pulled out his fingernails in an attempt to break his faith. Another time, they tied him to the ceiling fan by his hair and left him to hang there.

"Although I suffered greatly at the hands of my Muslim captors, I held no bitterness towards them. I knew that just a few years before, I had been one of them. I too had hated Christians.

"During my trial, I was found guilty of blasphemy. According to the *Sharia* law, I was to be executed by hanging. They tried to force me to recant my faith in Jesus. They assured me that if I cooperated there would be no more beatings, no more humiliation. I could go free.

"But I could not deny Jesus. Mohammed had never visited me; Jesus had. I knew He was the truth. I just prayed for the guards, hoping that they would also come to know Jesus."

On the day Zahid was to be hanged, he was unafraid of death as they came to take him from his cell. Even as they took him to the site of his scheduled execution and placed the noose around his neck, Zahid preached about Jesus to his guards and executioners. He wanted his last breath on earth to be used in telling his countryman that Jesus was "the way, the truth, and the life." Zahid stood ready to face his Savior.

Suddenly, loud voices were heard in the outer room. Guards hurried in to tell Zahid's executioners that the court had unexpectedly issued an order to release Zahid, stating that there was not enough evidence to execute him. To this day, no one knows why Zahid was suddenly allowed to go free.

Zahid later changed his name to Lazarus, feeling that he too had been raised from the dead. He traveled in the villages around his home testifying of his narrow escape from death. Many followers of Jesus did not trust him at first. But soon they saw his sincerity and received him into their family. They now assist him as he travels from village to village preaching Jesus as "the way, the truth, and the life."

"I live in a land ruled by the false teaching of Islam. My people are blinded, and I was chosen by God to be His voice. I count all that I have suffered nothing compared to the endless joy of knowing Jesus, the way, the truth, and the life."

—ZAHID[13]

Jesus Freaks in the Bible

Jeremiah: Standing Alone

It was more than 600 years before Jesus would be born. It was the time of the prophets, men and women God called to proclaim His message to His people. Jerusalem, the capital of Israel, was anything but the centerpiece of God's glory. The city was filled with people who worshipped idols, were sexually immoral, practiced fraud in their business dealings, and resorted to murder when things did not go their way.

In all of this, God was looking for even one good person, but found none. He stirred up a young man named Jeremiah, and asked him to speak forth a very unpopular message: God's judgment was on its way. Other so-called prophets were declaring God's blessing on Jerusalem; they were saying revival was coming. But God told Jeremiah to preach a different message.

"I will punish my people, because they are guilty of turning from me to worship idols," proclaimed God in Jeremiah 1:16 (CEV). And He sent this young man out to tell all the people of the punishment that was to come.

Needless to say, Jeremiah was not the most popular preacher of his day. The people liked what the other prophets told them—that they could keep doing whatever they wanted, and God would bless them. But Jeremiah told the truth. And the truth will often cost the one who tells it.

Jeremiah not only preached with words the message of God's impending judgment. He used object lessons to make his point as well. For instance, God instructed Jeremiah to buy a new pair of linen shorts, wear them for a while, then take them off and bury them between some large rocks. Some time later, Jeremiah was told to go retrieve the shorts, which by now had rotted and fallen apart. God told Jeremiah,

When I am finished with these people, they will be good for nothing, just like this pair of shorts. These shorts were tight around your waist, and that's how tightly I held onto the kingdoms of Israel and Judah. I wanted them to be my people. I wanted to make them famous, so that other nations would praise and honor me, but they refused to obey me.

—JEREMIAH 13: 10, 11 CEV

God also had Jeremiah smash a clay pot, showing that God would smash Israel for her sins. Jeremiah wore a wood and leather yoke to show that Israel was to submit to the rule of the Babylonians and he bought land from his cousin while the country was under siege by the Babylonians. God told Jeremiah to buy the land to show that His people would once again return to the land God promised His people.

These messages and the manner in which they were proclaimed were not well-received by the people in and around Jerusalem. They preferred to listen to the false prophets who told of great days of prosperity just around the corner. Jeremiah was put in jail under a trumped-up charge. When the foretold invasion by Israel's enemies came, Jeremiah resisted the urge to say, "I told you so." He chose to accompany his people to Babylon, where he spoke words of comfort, telling the Israelites that God would forgive them and once again bring them back to their land.

Jeremiah, even while a young man, took a stand that was very unpopular. He was persecuted by his own people for speaking the truth. But God promised to be by his side the whole time, and Jeremiah chose to obey God rather than seek the approval of others.

ChaPter SEVEN

Forgive
like a
JESUS
Freak

The woman slipped through the crowd toward the house where the great Man was dining. Other women on the street cast disapproving eyes on her and turned away in disgust. Men eyed her in a different way, as her painted face and anklet bells plainly told them who—and what—she was.

But today it didn't matter. She had heard about the Man from Galilee, and to think that He was right here in her town, eating with one of the temple leaders! The feast was already in progress when the woman entered, but she didn't care if she made a scene. She had to speak to Him.

When she saw Jesus, the words she'd wanted to say choked in her throat. Instead, she sank to the floor at His feet, sobbing quietly while the others stared. She took an alabaster jar from the folds of her robe and poured its contents—expensive, sweet-smelling perfume—on His feet, the oil mingling with her tears. Then she dried His feet with her long hair.

"Jesus, don't You know who this woman is?" the host cried out in a sharp tone. But instead of reprimanding the woman, Jesus had words for the host. "You did not put oil on My head, but she has poured oil on My feet. Her many sins have been forgiven, for she loved much. But he who has been forgiven little loves little."

Turning back to the woman, He said, "Your faith has saved you. Go in peace."

When a person becomes a Jesus Freak, something incredible happens in his heart. For some the change is instantaneous; for others it's a gradual process. But as we tune into God, He turns our anger into forgiveness, our selfishness into servanthood. Suddenly the status quo doesn't matter anymore. Instead, we find ourselves going against the flow, speaking kind words and doing deeds for nothing in return.

Love turns a self-seeker into a giver—and a forgiver.

Freely Received, Freely Given

Forgiveness is a rare commodity in our world. If we're honest, most of us will have to admit that we live by a modified version of the Golden Rule: Do unto others before they do unto you. Then it's open season for revenge! But that's the exact opposite of what Jesus told His followers to do. Listen to what He has to say on the subject of revenge:

As we **TUNE** into God, He **turns** our **anger** into forgiveness, our selfishness into servanthood.

"You have heard that the law of Moses says, 'If an eye is injured, injure the eye of the person who did it' . . . But I say, don't resist an evil person! If you are slapped on the right cheek, turn the other, too. . . . You have heard that the law of Moses says, 'Love your neighbor' and hate your enemy. But I say, love your enemies! Pray for those who persecute you! In that way, you will be acting as true children of your Father in heaven . . . If you love only those who love you, what good is that? . . . If you are kind only to your friends, how are you different from anyone else?"

—MATTHEW 5:38-39,43-47 NLT

Jesus said those words to a group of people gathered on a Galilean hillside 2,000 years ago, but He might as well be speaking straight to us today. Theologians have written whole books on the subject of the "hard sayings" of Jesus. This passage might qualify—it simply doesn't make sense to our natural mind. Why be kind to someone who curses at you when they pass you in the hall at school? Why offer to help that mean old woman who lives next door when you see her struggling to carry in a load of groceries?

Jesus Freaks may read these words of Christ and wince at first, but if we pause and allow them to sink into our spirit, something deep inside will click. Our spirit answers to the prodding of God's Spirit. Forgiving the unforgivable makes sense when we view the situation through Jesus' eyes. It's like everything else Jesus taught:

- If you want to live a meaningful life, you must "lose it" for Christ's sake.

- Don't worry about the "stuff" that consumes most people (money, clothes, and all that), but focus on God instead. He'll make sure you have the stuff you really need.

- Give, and you'll receive back more than you ever imagined. Withhold, and the little you have will slip through your fingers.

- Forgive, and you will be forgiven. Show mercy to others, and you'll be treated mercifully when the time comes.

Did you change dramatically once you became a Jesus Freak? You probably did, at least in the most obvious areas of your life. Or maybe you're still a little rough around the edges, in need of a good once-over with some sandpaper. No sweat. God is a thorough sander, and He promised to finish the work of art He's making you into. He's doing the same thing for each person you bump into. Allow Him to use you as His messenger of forgiveness.

The Hardest One to Forgive

The young man who had been in the audience that fateful day, named Saul of Tarsus, followed the mob. He stood a short distance away from the defendant, looking steadily at the sky as the crowd grew larger. The cries of the people were more heated now. A man handed Saul his coat, then stooped to pick up a stone as though waiting for a signal from Saul. Saul

lowered his gaze, then looked directly into the man's
eyes and nodded. It was time to silence the young
preacher—that Jesus Freak Stephen.

But Stephen wouldn't shut up. He continued
preaching despite the crowd's taunting, because the
Man he was telling them about was so important to
him. He couldn't stop talking about Him. Several
more men had now removed their coats, handed
them to Saul, and begun gathering rocks, many of
them so large that the men had to lift them with
two hands.

"This blasphemer must be dealt with."

"He speaks against Moses!"

"We don't want to hear about your Jesus anymore!"

A rock sailed past Stephen's head. He stopped
speaking long enough to duck it, dazed for a
moment, then stood to continue. The second rock
caught him near his temple, and he fell to his knees.
Another hit his shoulder. Then there were too many
to count.

Saul stroked his beard and watched through
slitted eyes as the stones rained down on Stephen,
draining the life from his body.

"No more Jesus talk!" someone yelled.

"Let this be a lesson to all who would proclaim
this Jesus!"

Stephen's clothes were torn by the blows, and
blood dripped freely from the tatters. He began to
pray, "Lord Jesus, receive my spirit." Then he scanned
the crowd until his eyes locked with those of the

What Saul didn't COUNT on was meeting GOD head-on.

young man who held a bundle of coats. "And Lord," he continued, "do not hold this sin against them."

When he said those words, Stephen died.

Slowly the men retrieved their coats from young Saul, who was soon left alone with the body of the young preacher. Saul had come to Jerusalem to help silence this growing craze about Jesus of Nazareth. Despite his hatred, he could not shake the young man's words and how fearlessly he had faced death. He stood staring at the body of the first martyr for this One they claimed was the Messiah. The glow that had so angered Saul was still on the young man's face. He had seen it as the smug pride of a heretic, but could it have been something else? He stifled the thought and turned away, more determined than ever to crush this Jesus movement.

What Saul didn't count on was meeting God head-on. As he journeyed down the road to Damascus, on yet another Jesus-busting mission, he was thrown to the ground and blinded by a light so bright it took a miracle to restore his sight. Most terrifying of all, out from the midst of the light came a Voice: *"Saul, Saul, why are you persecuting Me?"*

History (and those flannel-graph Bible stories you may have learned as a kid in Sunday school) tell us the rest of the story. This Jesus Freak persecutor named Saul became one of the greatest Jesus Freaks of all. He wrote most of the New Testament, and we know him today by the name of Paul—the apostle Paul.

But don't miss this very important point: Paul, like all of us, was *human* and had to live the rest of his life with the memory of how he tormented God's people. He openly calls himself "the least of the apostles" in Scripture. It's as if he's saying, "Hey, these other guys? They really walked and talked with Him. But who am I? By God's incredible grace I got to tag along and do the work He started through them. Blessed be His name forever."

Sometimes the hardest person to forgive is yourself.

Though you can be sure Satan taunted Paul with thoughts about his past, Paul learned what to do with those thoughts. He gives us a clue in the book of Philippians:

> *I once thought all these things were so very important, but now I consider them worthless because of what Christ has done . . . I have discarded everything else, counting it all as garbage, so that I may have Christ and become one with him. I no longer count on my own goodness or my ability to obey God's law, but I trust Christ to save me. . . . I don't mean to say that I have already achieved these things or that I have already reached perfection! But I keep working toward that day when I will finally be all that Christ Jesus saved me for and wants me to be. No, dear brothers and sisters, I am still not all I should be, but I am focusing all my energies on this one thing: Forgetting the past and looking forward to what lies ahead, I strain to reach the end of the race and receive the prize for which God, through Christ Jesus, is calling us up to heaven.*

—PHILIPPIANS 3:7-9,12-14 NLT

Freedom is FOUND in forgiveness—**of others,** and of **yourself.**

Freedom is found in forgiveness—of others and of yourself. No, you may not totally forget the deeds of the past, but God can make something good come out of those years you thought were lost. And over time you'll find that the memory of those shameful things will grow dimmer as He pulls you into the wonderful plan He called you to fulfill—the life you were destined to live as a Jesus Freak!

How can you let go of your feelings toward those
who have hurt you?

Think of three people who infuriate you. Now
picture them through the eyes of Jesus, and stop to
pray for them, even if it feels awkward at first. (Hint:
If you're stuck, try a simple "Lord, bless them"
prayer. It'll get easier every time you pray!)

Jesus Freaks Around You Now

We Were with Christ
Richard Wurmbrand, Romania, 1945

One by one, the priests and pastors of Romania stood and offered words of praise for Communism and declared their loyalty to the new regime . . . it was a year after the Communists had seized power in Romania. The government had invited all religious leaders to attend a congress at the Parliament building, and more than 4,000 attended. First, they chose Joseph Stalin as honorary president of the congress. Then the speeches began. It was absurd and horrible. Communism was dedicated to the destruction of religion, as had already been shown in Russia. Yet bishops and pastors arose and declared that Communism and Christianity were fundamentally the same and could coexist. Out of fear, these men of God were filling the air with flattery and lies.

It was as if they spat in Jesus Christ's face.

Sabina Wurmbrand could stand it no longer. She whispered to her husband, "Richard, stand up and wash away this shame from the face of Christ."

Richard knew what would happen: "If I speak, you will lose your husband."

Sabina replied, "I do not wish to have a coward for a husband."

Pastor Wurmbrand took the stage. To everyone's surprise, he began to preach . . . After this Richard Wurmbrand was a marked man.

On Sunday, February 29, 1948, Pastor Wurmbrand was on his way to church when he was kidnapped by a small group of secret police. He tells what happened next:

"I was led to a prison thirty feet beneath the earth where I was kept in solitary confinement. For years, I was kept alone in a cell. Never did I see the sun, moon, stars, flowers. Never did I see a man except the interrogators who beat and tortured me. Never did I have a book, never a bit of paper. When after many years I had to write again, I could not even remember how to write a capital D.

". . . When we were first put in solitary confinement, it was like dying. Every one of us lived again his past sins and his neglects of duties. We all had an unimaginable pain in our hearts, thinking that we had not done our utmost for the Highest, for the One who has given His life for us on the Cross.

"I was in the depths of this remorse and pain, when suddenly, the wall of the jail began to shine like diamonds. I have seen many beautiful things, but never have I seen the beauties which I have seen in the dark cell beneath the earth. Never have I heard such beautiful music as on that day.

"The King of kings, Jesus, was with us. We saw His understanding, loving eyes. He wiped our tears away. He sent us words of love and words of forgiveness. We knew that everything which had been evil in our lives had passed away, had been forgotten by God. Now there came wonderful days; the bride was in the arms of the Bridegroom—*we were with Christ.*

"We no longer believed about God and Christ and angels because Bible verses said it. We didn't remember Bible verses anymore. We remembered about God because we experienced it. With great humility we can say with the apostles, 'What we have seen with our eyes, what we have heard with our ears, what we have touched with our own fingers, this we tell to you.'

". . . And then the miracle happened. When it was at the worst, when we were tortured as never before, we began to love those who tortured us. Just as a flower, when you bruise it under your foot, rewards you with its perfume, the more we were mocked and tortured, the more we pitied and loved our torturers."

Many have asked Wurmbrand, "How can you love someone who is torturing you?" He replies:

"By looking at men . . . not as they are, but as they will be . . . I could also see in our persecutors a Saul of Tarsus—a future apostle Paul. Many officers of the secret police to whom we witnessed became Christians and were happy to later suffer in prison for having found our Christ. Although we were whipped, as Paul was, in our jailers we saw the potential of the jailer in Philippi who became a convert. We dreamed that soon they would ask, 'What must I do to be saved?'"

When Pastor Wurmbrand was released in 1956, he resumed his work with the underground church. In 1959, he was turned over to the authorities again, this time by one of his own co-workers. He was released the second time in 1964, and again resumed his work.

In 1967, the Wurmbrands formally started their mission to the Communists, which was called Jesus to the Communist World. Today, this ministry is known as The Voice of the Martyrs. Both Richard and Sabina have gone to be with the Lord in recent years, but their work, a ministry dedicated to serving the persecuted church wherever it may be found, continues.[14]

Jesus Freaks in the Bible

Mary Magdalene: Ashamed No More

Most men looked at her with a leering glance, or one of those sweeping head-to-toe looks that broadcast to the world what she was—a prostitute, a painted woman, a whore.

But *this* Man looked at her in a different way.

When Jesus of Nazareth came to town, news spread quickly that He would be dining at the home of a Pharisee. Mary heard the stories about Him. Some called Him a prophet. Others called Him Rabbi—teacher. Whatever He was, she hoped He could help her. Her life of shame had taken its toll. She was ready to make a change. She just needed someone to show her how.

Tucking a vial of perfume in her robes, she slipped through the crowds and made her way to the Pharisee's house. There He was, seated at the center of the table where all eyes could focus on Him.

Made bold by her desperation, Mary fell at His feet and started crying. She poured the perfumed oil on His feet and then dried them with her hair. That was when He did it—He lifted her chin so she was forced to look Him in the eyes.

Such eyes they were! She had never seen eyes so full of tenderness before. Godly tenderness. "Your sins are forgiven," He said simply. And at that moment she knew she was truly free for the first time in her life.

Mary felt a little awkward when she started attending Jesus Freak meetings, but the other women accepted her as if she was one of them. "You *are* one of us!" somebody told her one day. The truth of that statement sank in, and she relished it: She was a Jesus-follower, a Jesus Freak!

She was also one of the first Jesus Freaks to see Jesus after He rose from the dead. And for that, along with her shame-to-salvation story, she is most remembered today.

ChaPter EIGHT

Rejoice
like a
JESUS
Freak

The queen stared out the window and despised what she saw—her husband, stripped of his kingly clothes, dancing bare-chested in the streets like a commoner. Like a drunk. Did he have no shame? She let the curtain fall back across the window and turned away.

King David led the procession as the Ark of the Covenant was returned to Jerusalem. This sacred box, which held the stone tablets Moses had brought down from Mount Sinai, was being carted to its rightful place at last. This was cause for joy. It was cause for celebration. It was cause for dancing!

Trumpets blared, the people shouted, and David danced before the Lord as the procession wound its way into the city. His heart was filled to bursting, overflowing in this outward expression of childlike joy. God saw him and was pleased. God saw Michal's reaction and was displeased.

They brought the ark of the LORD and set it in its place inside the tent that David had pitched for it, and David sacrificed burnt offerings and fellowship offerings before the LORD . . . When David returned home to bless his household, Michal daughter of Saul came out to meet him and said, "How the king of Israel has distinguished himself today, disrobing in the sight of the slave girls of his servants as any vulgar fellow would!"

David said to Michal, "It was before the LORD, who chose me rather than your father or anyone from his house when he appointed me ruler over the LORD's people Israel—I will celebrate before the LORD. I will become even more undignified than this, and I will be humiliated in my own eyes. But by these slave girls you spoke of, I will be held in honor."

And Michal daughter of Saul had no children to the day of her death.

—2 SAMUEL 6:17,20-23

God revels in the childlike joy of His people. Jesus Freaks aren't ashamed to be fools for God. Like David, they're more concerned with what God thinks than what other people think—even if it means they look silly in the process.

Have you ever been so happy you couldn't contain your joy? Maybe it bubbled up in the form of spontaneous laughter. Maybe it spilled onto your features in a contagious smile. Maybe you hopped and danced. Or perhaps you felt so exhilarated you went for a run, taking the road in long strides rather than your usual mid-tempo jog. Somehow, you had to *express* that inner feeling of perfect happiness, you just had to get it out!

God revels in the childlike JOY of His people.

*Though you have not seen him, you love him; and
even though you do not see him now, you believe in him
and are filled with an inexpressible and glorious joy, for
you are receiving the goal of your faith, the salvation of
your souls.*

Peter the Apostle
Martyred in Rome, 65 A.D.
1 PETER 1:8-9

The Real Deal

Most people have had happy times in their lives.
And many would describe themselves as basically
happy individuals. But did you know there's a big
difference between happiness and joy? Happiness is
a feel-good feeling. It ebbs and flows with the
circumstances of our lives. *We land that job we've
been trying so hard for. But then . . . A close friend gets
killed by a drunken driver.* Often our happiness
depends on how we're treated by those around us.
*She loves me, she loves me not! He wants me, he wants
me not!* No wonder happiness is such an elusive
thing. Just when we think we have it in our grasp, it
slips through our fingers.

Joy, on the other hand, is a deep sense of peace
and well-being that lives in our spirit. True joy—the
kind that comes only from God—doesn't come and go.
It lodges within us and holds us steady on our course.
It's our "true north" as we navigate through life.

Happiness shows on a face, but joy emanates
from the spirit. You can see it in a Jesus Freak's eyes,
since eyes are the window of the soul.

True JOY—the kind that **COMES** only from God—**doesn't come** and go.

On the night of January 6, 1850, a blizzard hit England, causing a young man named Charles to duck into a tiny church close to his home rather than venture out to the church he usually attended. Inside, a handful of people stood around the stove, huddling close for warmth. A man read from Isaiah 45:22—*"Look unto me, and be ye saved, all the ends of the earth"*—and the words found their mark on at least one person that night. When the tiny gathering broke up, the young man headed for home, his heart blazing with a strange new fire.

Years later, the young man—now the great preacher Charles Spurgeon—wrote, "As the snow fell on my road home from the little house of prayer, I thought every snowflake talked with me and told of the pardon I had found." When he stepped through the door, his mother saw his countenance and said, "Something wonderful has happened to you!"

Jesus Freaks can't keep their joy hidden.

You are the light of the world—like a city on a mountain, glowing in the night for all to see. Don't hide your light under a basket! Instead, put it on a stand and let it shine for all. In the same way, let your good deeds shine out for all to see, so that everyone will praise your heavenly Father.

—MATTHEW 5:14-16 NLT

The Good Life

Everybody wants a good life. We even joke about living "the good life." But Jesus promised His followers not necessarily a good life, but an *abundant* life. Webster's defines *abundant* as "more than enough; amply sufficient; bountiful."[15] Translated into Jesus Freak terminology, that means God promises to give us not only everything we truly need but also an endless well of peace and joy to draw from. If you are a Jesus Freak, the life God has planned for you goes beyond even your wildest dreams. He wants to take you on a wild ride that centers on trusting Him, obeying Him, and following His lead. What will it cost you? Everything—your heart, your time, your willingness, your money, your reputation, maybe even your life. But remember: In exchange for "losing your life," you get a major upgrade. You gain His peace, His joy, His supernatural power, His perfect plan here and now, and a never-ending future with Him in heaven.

Jesus knew when the time had come for Him to die. During one of His last conversations on earth, He told His disciples:

I'm telling you these things while I'm still living with you. The Friend, the Holy Spirit whom the Father will send at my request, will make everything plain to you. He will remind you of all the things I have told you. I'm leaving you well and whole. That's my parting gift to you. Peace. I don't leave you the way you're used to being left—feeling abandoned, bereft. So don't be upset. Don't be distraught . . .

I've told you these things for a purpose: that my joy might be your joy, and your joy wholly mature. This is my command: Love one another the way I loved you.

*This is the very best way to love. Put your life on the
line for your friends.*

—John 14:25-27,15:9-13, The Message

Supernatural Strength

It doesn't take a rocket scientist to figure out
something is very wrong with the idea of a good God
overseeing a suffering world. If He exists, then why
does He allow such horrible things to happen? It's a
question as old as humanity itself. The only answer
is that this isn't the way God intended things to be.
We humans messed things up, and now we are
paying the price for it.

But Jesus Freaks have a secret weapon against
the horrors of this world: Jesus Himself! When He
comes to make His "home" in your spirit, it truly is
His home. And He will protect what is His. He
doesn't promise to make your life easier, but He
changes the way you view that life and gives you
supernatural strength to make it through the hard
times. Suddenly your perspective is filtered through
His eyes, His heart, His gentle Spirit, His joy.

A baby girl named Fanny, born in a small New
York town in 1820, contracted a cold in her eyes
when she was just six weeks old. A country doctor
prescribed the wrong treatment, and the little girl
was left blind for life. As she grew up, she determined to make the best of her disability, writing at
age eight: "O what a happy soul I am! Although I

cannot see, I am resolved that in this world contented I will be."

Fanny went on to a career as a teacher and writer-in-residence at New York's Institute for the Blind. She recited her poems before Congress and made friends with powerful people, including presidents.

But something was missing from her life. In 1851, she found the missing piece: a relationship with Jesus Christ. Fourteen years later, she was introduced to the hymnist William Bradbury, who encouraged her to turn her poems into hymns. Bradbury gave Fanny the idea for a song he needed, and she sat down to write her very first hymn: *We are going, we are going / To a home beyond the skies / Where the fields are robed in beauty / And the sunlight never dies.*

It was the first of more than 8,000 hymns written by Fanny Crosby. Perhaps her most famous hymn, "To God Be the Glory," goes like this:

> *To God be the glory, great things*
>   *He has done;*
> *So loved He the world that He*
>   *gave us His Son,*
> *Who yielded His life an atonement*
>   *for sin,*
> *And opened the life gate that all*
>   *may go in.*
>
> *Praise the Lord, praise the Lord,*
> *Let the earth hear His voice!*
> *Praise the Lord, praise the Lord,*
> *Let the people rejoice!*

O come to the Father, through
  Jesus the Son,
And give Him the glory, great
  things He has done.
Great things He has taught us,
  great things He has done,
And great our rejoicing through
  Jesus the Son;
But purer, and higher, and
  greater will be
Our wonder, our transport,
  when Jesus we see.

Another of Fanny Crosby's best-known hymns, "Blessed Assurance," contains the words: *This is my story, this is my song / Praising my Savior, all the day long . . . / Perfect submission, all is at rest / I in my Savior am happy and blest / Watching and waiting, looking above / Filled with His goodness, lost in His love.*

Though we might look at Fanny Crosby's story and see a life filled with hardship and sadness, she found a reason to sing out for joy. It was the supernatural joy of a Jesus Freak!

Make 'em Curious!

A Jesus Freak whose joy overflows is a puzzling thing to a watching world. But that's not a bad thing. Let your light make 'em curious! Let people see your peace under pressure and wonder what your secret is. Maybe they'll work up the courage to ask you about it. Joy in the midst of suffering always confounds those who don't possess it.

One day, on the way to visit some friends, Englishman John Denley was stopped and searched by the authorities, who found his written confession of faith. Denley believed the church was built upon the apostles and prophets, with Christ as its head. He also believed that the present state of the church, the Church of England in the 1500s, was not part of this true Church. At that time, many of its teachings were contrary to the Bible.

For his beliefs he was turned over to a local government official, who turned him over to the bishop for questioning. Denley would not back down from his statement of faith, so he was condemned to die.

Within six weeks he was sent to the stake to be burned. When they lit the wood beneath him, Denley showed no fear. He cheerfully sang a psalm as the flames rose around him. One of his tormentors picked up a piece of wood and threw it at him, hitting him in the face. He hoped to anger or silence Denley, but Denley only responded, "Truly, you have spoiled a good old song." Then he spread his arms again and continued singing until he died.

"Count yourselves blessed every time people put you down or throw you out or speak lies about you to discredit me. What it means is that the truth is too close for comfort and they are uncomfortable. You can be glad when that happens—give a cheer, even!—for though they don't like it, I do! And all heaven applauds."

Jesus Christ
MATTHEW 5:11-12 THE MESSAGE

Let **your**
LIGHT
make 'em
curious!

Another sixteenth-century Englishman also found a reason to rejoice through his hardships. And, like Denley, he was willing to give his life for the sake of the gospel.

John Bradford stood boldly before the Lord Chancellor. "I urge you," the young man said, "don't condemn the innocent. If you believe I am guilty, you should pass sentence on me. If not, you should set me free."

Bradford, the well-loved pastor of St. Paul's in London, was thrown into prison for his beliefs that differed from the state church during Queen Mary's reign. While he was in prison, so many of his congregation came to visit him that he continued to preach twice a day. He also preached weekly to the other men in prison, the thieves and common criminals, exhorting them from the Word of God and often giving them money to buy food.

Bradford's keepers trusted him so much that he was often allowed to leave the prison unescorted to visit sick members of his congregation. All he had to do was to promise that he would return by a certain hour. He was so careful about keeping his word that he was usually back well before his curfew.

After a year and a half, Bradford was offered a pardon if he would deny his beliefs, but he would not. Then after six more months in prison, the offer was repeated. Again he refused.

"John," his friends warned, "you need to do something to stall for more time. Ask to discuss your religious beliefs with Queen Mary's learned men. That will take you out of immediate danger."

John replied, "If I did that, the people would think I have begun to doubt the doctrine I confess. I don't doubt it at all."

"Then they will probably kill you very soon," his friends said sadly.

The very next day John was sentenced to death, and the keeper's wife came to him with the news: "Tomorrow you will be burned."

Bradford looked to heaven and said, "I thank God for it. I have waited for this for a long time. Lord, make me worthy of this."

Hoping to keep the crowds from knowing what was going on, the guards transferred him to another prison in the middle of the night. But somehow the word got out, and a great multitude came to bid him farewell. Many wept openly as they prayed for him. Bradford, in return, gently said farewell and prayed for them and their future.

At 4 A.M. the next day, a large crowd had gathered at the place where Bradford was to be burned. Finally, at 9 A.M., an unusually large number of heavily armed men brought Bradford out to the stake. With him was John Leaf, a teenager, who also refused to deny his faith. Both men fell flat to the ground and prayed for an hour.

Bradford got up, kissed a piece of firewood, and then kissed the stake itself. In a loud voice he spoke to the crowd: "England, repent of your sins! Beware of idolatry. Beware of false teachers. See they don't deceive you!" Then he forgave his persecutors and asked the crowd to pray with him.

Turning his head toward John Leaf, he said, "Be of good comfort, brother, for we shall have a merry supper with the Lord tonight!"

What is the difference between joy and happiness?

We are told in Nehemiah 8:10 that God's joy is our
strength. How can joy be strength when all around
us is terror or sadness?

Jesus Freaks Around You Now

Jubilant Dance for Jesus
Russian captain, Romania, 1940s

"Christianity has become dramatic with us,"
wrote Pastor Richard Wurmbrand, a leader of the
underground church in Communist Romania.
"When Christians in free countries win a soul for
Christ, the new believer may become a member of a
quietly living church. But when those in captive
nations win someone, we know that he may have to
go to prison and that his children may become
orphans. The joy of having brought someone to
Christ is always mixed with this feeling that there is
a price that must be paid.

"When I was still living behind the Iron Curtain,
I had met a Russian captain. He loved God, he
longed after God, but he had never seen a Bible. He
had never attended religious services. He had no religious education, but he loved God without the
slightest knowledge of Him.

"I read to him the Sermon on the Mount and the
parables of Jesus. After hearing them, he danced
around the room in rapturous joy, proclaiming,
'What a wonderful beauty! How could I live without
knowing this Christ?' It was the first time that I saw
someone jubilating in Christ.

"Then I made a mistake. I read to him the passion
and crucifixion of Christ, without having prepared
him for this. He had not expected it. When he heard
how Christ was beaten, how He was crucified, and

that in the end He died, he fell in an armchair and began to weep bitterly. He had believed in a Savior and now his Savior was dead!

"I looked at him and was ashamed that I had called myself a Christian and a pastor, a teacher of others. I had never shared the sufferings of Christ as this Russian officer now shared them. Looking at him was, for me, like seeing Mary Magdalene weeping at the foot of the cross or at the empty tomb.

"Then I read to him the story of the resurrection. When he heard this wonderful news, that the Savior arose from the tomb, he slapped his knees, and shouted for joy: 'He is alive! He is alive!' Again he danced around the room, overwhelmed with happiness.

"I said to him, 'Let us pray.'

"He fell on his knees together with me. He did not know our holy phrases. His words of prayer were, 'O God, what a fine chap You are! If I were You and You were me, I would never have forgiven You Your sins. But You are really a very nice chap! I love You with all my heart.'

"I think that all the angels in heaven stopped what they were doing to listen to this sublime prayer from this Russian officer. When this man received Christ, he knew he would immediately lose his position as an officer, that prison and perhaps death in jail would almost surely follow. He gladly paid the price. He was ready to lose everything."[16]

ChaPter **NINE**

Serve

like a

JESUS

Freak

But among you, those who are the greatest should take the lowest rank, and the leader should be like a servant.

—LUKE 22:26 NLT

Jesse Brand was still a young man in 1907 when he made the decision to go to India as a medical missionary. Single, and single-minded, he journeyed there alone. But he was not alone for too long. Back home in England, a girl named Evelyn Harris was the undisputed "babe" of her upscale London crowd. Even so, she chose to abandon her glamorous life, travel to India, and marry Jesse in 1913.

The couple lived in the Chat Mountains, where flea-covered rats swarmed through the villages spreading disease. Jesse and Evelyn gave medical aid to the villagers and organized programs to help the local farmers make a better living. They talked about Jesus to everybody they came in contact with. In one year alone, Jesse preached 4,000 times in ninety villages. As new believers popped up, the Brands started new churches to train believers in the Scriptures.

When their son, Paul, was born, Jesse and Evelyn were determined to raise him with a love for God, for nature, and for India. Evelyn taught her son in the shade of a tamarind tree, and Jesse often took Paul on long nature walks, teaching him to see God in the wonders around him. At age nine, Paul was sent to England to be educated.

Over the years, the Brands continued providing medical aid to the Indian villagers. In 1928 Jesse developed blackwater fever, yet he managed to preach with a 104-degree temperature. For his sermon that day he chose a passage from Isaiah 60: *Stand up! Shine! Your new day is dawning. The glory of the* LORD *shines brightly on you. The earth and its people are covered with darkness, but the glory of the* LORD *is shining upon you. Nations and kings will come to the light of your dawning day* (Isaiah 60:1-3 CEV).

Two days later, Jesse's temperature reached 106. Evelyn sat by his bed and watched her husband slowly die. She had worked by his side for fifteen years, and now she planned to carry on that work alone.

Meanwhile, word of his father's death reached fourteen-year-old Paul in England. Within a day or two, a letter from his father—his last—arrived from India. In it, Jesse wrote: *". . . and always be looking to God with thankfulness and worship for having placed you in such a delightful corner of the universe as the planet Earth."*

Years later, legends told of an old woman the villagers called "Granny Brand" who could be seen hiking over the mountains with her walking stick. She lived to see her son, Dr. Paul Brand, became a famous missionary doctor specializing in the treatment of leprosy.

Radical Service

Jesus Freaks are known for doing crazy things— like good deeds for no reward, putting other people before themselves, and talking about a Man who lived 2,000 years ago. Such a lifestyle raises quite a few questions, and usually eyebrows too. *What's the motivation?* people wonder. *There's gotta be a catch. Nobody does things "just because."* But that's exactly what makes Christianity stand apart from all the other religions of the world. The words of Jesus shook up the world when He walked the earth, and they're still shaking things up today.

> *God blesses those who realize their need for him,*
> *for the Kingdom of Heaven is given to them.*
> *God blesses those who mourn,*
> *for they will be comforted.*
> *God blesses those who are gently and lowly,*
> *for the whole earth will belong to them.*
> *God blesses those who are hungry and thirsty*
>   *for justice,*
> *for they will receive it in full.*
> *God blesses those who are merciful,*

for they will be shown mercy.
God blesses those whose hearts are pure,
for they will see God.
God blesses those who work for peace,
for they will be called the children of God.
God blesses those who are persecuted because
they live for God,
for the Kingdom of Heaven is theirs.

—MATTHEW 5:3-12 NLT

The WORDS of Jesus shook up the world when He WALKED the earth, and they're still shaking things up today.

The world has a shortage of people who want to make a difference—especially the "God" kind of difference. Even Jesus Freaks sometimes get lazy and lose their focus on the things that really matter. What's the cure for this type of apathy? "Losing yourself" on a daily basis and training yourself to look for opportunities to serve. Most likely, you'll find that serving God is addictive.

There are several ways you can get involved:

- *Go on a short-term missions trip.* A typical trip lasts one to two weeks and may use street evangelism, drama, music, humanitarian aid, or other means to reach people for Christ. In most cases, you're required to raise the money to pay your own way for the trip. A good place to start is with your church or youth group. Write a letter to the pastor, telling him about your decision to go on the missions trip (include a brochure from the missions organization so he knows your request is legitimate). He may post the letter in the church bulletin, asking for donations on your behalf. Or you can write or call your close friends and relatives with the same request. Although it may seem awkward asking for money, you'll probably be surprised at the way God provides the funds you need for the trip. Whenever we work for Him, He takes care of our needs. Many organizations provide Jesus Freaks the opportunity to get out there and deliver the gospel to people who've never heard it. These include YWAM, Teen Mania Ministries, Adventures in Missions, Real Impact Missions, and Campus Crusade for Christ. Here are the Web sites for each:

http://www.ywam.org/

http://www.teenmania.org/

http://www.adventures.org/shortterm/ groups/index.html

http://www.realimpact.com/

http://www.ccci.org/

- *Help serve the abused, homeless, and needy in your hometown.* Most communities have humanitarian organizations that are desperate for helping hands. Soup kitchens, crisis pregnancy centers, jails, homeless shelters, suicide intervention centers, shelters for battered women and children—the list goes on and on. Check in the Yellow Pages under Human Services Organizations or Social Services Organizations, or ask your youth pastor for the names of local ministries you can help. Your task may be as mundane as sorting donated clothes for a homeless shelter or as personal as praying with someone who tried to kill herself a day ago. Remember: It all counts with God. He sees the time, effort, and love you put into folding huge stacks of clothes, and He sees the person with a broken heart who catches a glimmer of hope when you pray for them.

- *Give your money to God.* How does a person actually give money to God? You can't exactly write a check to the Almighty, and He doesn't accept debit cards! But the churches, ministries, and organizations that work on His behalf do. Whenever we give money to keep God's work afloat, He blesses us more than we expected. The blessing may not come in material or financial ways, but you can be sure it will come.

God takes delight in joyful givers. The world operates by a "what's-in-it-for-me?" motive. By contrast, a Jesus Freak thinks, *What's in it for God?* Here's the way Jesus said His followers should think about money:

> *"You can't worship two gods at once. Loving one god, you'll end up hating the other. Adoration of one feeds contempt for the other. You can't worship God and Money both. If you decide for God, living a life of God-worship, it follows that you don't fuss about what's on the table at mealtimes or whether the clothes in your*

G o d TAKES delight in joyful givers.

closet are in fashion. There is far more to your life than the food you put in your stomach, more to your outer appearance than the clothes you hang on your body . . . Instead of looking at the fashions, walk out into the fields and look at the wildflowers. They never primp or shop, but have you ever seen color and design quite like it? The ten best dressed men and women in the country look shabby alongside them.

If God gives such attention to the appearance of wildflowers—most of which are never even seen—don't you think he'll attend to you, take pride in you, do his best for you? . . . What I'm trying to do here is to get you to relax, to not be so preoccupied with getting, so you can respond to God's giving. People who don't know God and the way he works fuss over these things, but you know both God and how he works. Steep your life in God-reality, God-initiative, God-provisions. Don't worry about missing out. You'll find all your everyday human concerns will be met."

—MATTHEW 6:24-25,28-33 THE MESSAGE

Did you know that financial giving is the one area in which God *asks* you to test Him? He must have known we'd be challenged in this area. Listen to what He spoke through the Old Testament prophet Malachi: *"Will a man rob God? Yet you rob me. But you ask, 'How do we rob you?' In tithes and offerings. You are under a curse . . . because you are robbing me. Bring the whole tithe [one-tenth of your income] into the storehouse, that there may be food in my house. 'Test me in this,' says the LORD Almighty, 'and see if I will not throw open the floodgates of heaven*

*and pour out so much blessing that you will not have
room enough for it'"* (Malachi 3:8-10).

In addition to local ministries, national and
international ministries need your help too. If you
can't physically be a part of their outreaches, take
part through your wallet. Many ministries help the
persecuted church around the world, such as The
Voice of the Martyrs, Open Doors with Brother
Andrew, and Samaritan's Purse. Your money provides
Bibles translated into foreign languages, food, clothing, medical supplies, gospel films, and practical
support for the families of the persecuted. It also
helps to send other workers to these regions.

A Miracle in the Mail

Hudson Taylor had decided that his ministry,
China Inland Mission, would never solicit money
but would trust God to supply its needs. In a letter
dated November 18, 1857, Taylor described one
miracle of provision:

**Many seem to think I am very poor.
This is true enough in one sense, but I
thank God it is "as poor, yet making many
rich." My God shall supply all my needs;
to him be the glory. I would not, if I
could, be otherwise than I am—entirely
dependent myself upon the Lord, and
used as a channel of help to others.**

On Saturday we supplied, as usual, breakfast to the destitute poor, who came to the number of 70. Sometimes they do not reach 40, at other times exceeding 80 . . . Well, on that Saturday morning we paid all expenses, and provided ourselves for the morrow, after which we had not a single dollar left between us. How the Lord was going to provide for Monday we knew not; but over our mantelpiece hung two scrolls in the Chinese character—Ebenezer, "Hitherto hath the Lord helped us"; and Jehovah-Jireh, "The Lord will provide"—and he kept us from doubting for a moment. That very day the mail came in, a week sooner than was expected, and Mr. Jones received $214. We thanked God and took courage. On Monday the poor had their breakfast as usual, for we had not told them not to come, being assured that it was the Lord's work, and that the Lord would provide. We could not help our eyes filling with tears of gratitude when we saw not only our own needs supplied, but the widow and the orphan, the blind and the lame, the friendless and the destitute, together provided for by the bounty of Him who feeds the ravens.

When we're bold enough to risk our own welfare for God, He sets into motion—on our behalf—the same supernatural power that created the universe. And don't be surprised if He uses extraordinary means to supply your ordinary needs! In fact, God seems to specialize in surprises like this.

If you could talk to John Craig, a Scotsman who lived during the 1500s, he'd tell you the amazing story of how God took care of him on three separate occasions.

Condemned to death for believing the true gospel, rather than the church's corrupt teachings, Craig was hauled to Rome and thrown into prison, where he waited for his turn at the stake. But on the evening before his scheduled execution, news arrived that the pope had died. According to Roman custom, all prisoners were temporarily released until a new pope could be appointed.

Seizing the moment, Craig escaped to an inn just outside the city. A group of soldiers tracked him down, but the captain of the guard hesitated when he saw Craig's face. Years earlier, Craig had helped a wounded soldier. "I am the man you relieved," the captain said, "and providence has now put it into my power to return the kindness—you are at liberty." Handing Craig all the money he had in his pockets, the captain drew a map showing an escape route and sent Craig on his way.

Guided by the captain's map, and aided by his money, Craig trekked through Italy on foot, sticking to the lesser-known routes and buying food whenever he could. Eventually, though, his money ran out, and Craig lay down in the woods—exhausted and depressed. *Now how would he survive?* he wondered.

Just then the sound of footsteps snapping through the undergrowth broke his thoughts. Craig tensed, ready to flee.

It was only a dog—carrying a purse in its mouth. Craig waved the dog away, assuming it was some kind of a trick. But the dog came up and dropped the purse in his lap, then disappeared.

Inside Craig found enough money to reach Austria, where he appealed to the emperor for help. When he finally made it back to Scotland, he preached the gospel of Jesus Christ for the rest of his life.

My life is worth nothing unless I use it for doing the work assigned me by the Lord Jesus—the work of telling others the Good News about God's wonderful kindness and love.

Paul the Apostle

Martyred in Rome, 65 A.D.

ACTS 20:24 NLT

For we do not want you to be unaware, brethren, of our affliction which came to us in Asia, that we were burdened excessively, beyond our strength, so that we despaired even of life; indeed we had the sentence of death within ourselves in order that we should not trust in ourselves, but in God who raises the dead; who delivered us from so great a peril of death, and will deliver us...you also joining in helping us through your prayers, that thanks may be given by many persons on

our behalf for the favor bestowed upon us through the
prayers of many.

Paul the Apostle

Martyred in Rome, 65 A.D.

2 CORINTHIANS 1:8-11 NAS

A life of serving God is a life well lived. If you've
been sitting on the sidelines, waiting for the perfect
time to jump in the game, don't wait any longer. Just
make yourself available—God will show you what to
do and where to go.

In what specific way can you become a radical
servant of Jesus Christ?

Are you trying to keep God and money on equal
playing fields?

When you give to God, what's the motive behind
your giving?

What will happen if you go out on a limb and trust
God with your money?

How can you turn your focus toward others and
away from yourself?

Jesus Freaks Around You Now

A Decision to Stay
To Dinh Trung
Vietnam, 1995

They came without warning, out of nowhere.

Evangelist To Dinh Trung was riding his bike over a rough dirt road in North Vietnam. The ruts in the road demanded his full attention. Suddenly he was surrounded by a squad of Communist police officers who pulled him off his bicycle and started beating him. They made fun of him in front of the crowd of villagers, videotaping everything. Finally, he was taken to prison and kept there without a trial.

Trung had traveled hundreds of miles on his bike while ministering to the K'Ho tribe. Dozens of K'Ho villagers had become Jesus-followers after Trung visited them in their homes. But the K'Ho is one of sixty tribes in Vietnam that the government has strictly forbidden Jesus Freaks to evangelize. Still, more and more believers have dedicated themselves to take the good news of the gospel "outside the camp," where no official churches exist. Some are schoolteachers; most are rice farmers or fishermen. All are persecuted by the Communist government.

Trung was in prison for six months before his trial. He saw this as a divine opportunity to preach to the lost. What else could the Communists do to him? He was already in prison! Through his efforts, many have come to Christ in the prison near Quang Ngai.

Meanwhile, Jesus Freaks around the world were alerted to Trung's situation. Many prayed and wrote letters on his behalf. Because of the pressure put on Vietnamese authorities, Trung was offered an early release. The only problem: The evangelist wasn't ready to leave! He felt God's call to stay in prison and disciple his new flock of believers. Trung refused his early release and chose to serve his full sentence.

Trung was greatly encouraged when he heard of the many letters written by believers on his behalf. He knows he is called to be an evangelist in Vietnam—which is a very dangerous occupation. The prayers and letters gave him the strength to continue to be a witness to his fellow inmates for the kingdom of God.

"I don't care about my own life. The most important thing is that I complete my mission, the work that the Lord Jesus gave me—to tell people the good news about God's grace."[17]

Jesus Freaks in the Bible

Peter: The "Rock" That Ate Crow

Loud, brash, arrogant—those were good adjectives to describe Peter. Yet Jesus saw past this rough exterior to the man he would be someday. From the very start, when Peter threw down his fishing nets and followed Jesus, he was a natural leader. Some of the other disciples were big, strapping men, but none were quite like Peter. His name meant "rock." When Peter spoke, people listened. Peter said what he meant and meant what he said—most of the time.

That's why no one was surprised when he blurted out that he would never deny the Lord, no matter what the others did. "Peter, before the rooster crows tomorrow morning, you will deny Me three times," Jesus said, the sadness showing in His eyes.

Peter couldn't believe his ears. Not him! Not the boldest of the disciples. "Lord, I'll never betray You!" he insisted.

Things were heating up in Jerusalem. The religious leaders wanted Jesus dead. That night the twelve disciples would celebrate the Passover meal with their Master. It would be their last meal with Him, but no one knew that except Jesus.

When Judas slipped out, offering some lame excuse to get away, the others barely noticed. They continued eating. Later, Jesus led the eleven remaining men into a garden to pray with Him. He knew His time of death was fast approaching.

There in the garden, led by Judas himself, a group of soldiers arrested Jesus. Most of the disciples scattered. But not Peter. Peter was brave. He followed at a distance to see where the soldiers were taking his Lord.

Then a strange thing happened. Fear seized Peter. Being associated with Jesus meant certain death. He kept to the shadows as he edged his way to the high priest's house. Three different people accused him of being a Jesus-follower, and all three times Peter denied it. As he shouted out the last "No!" Jesus turned and looked into his eyes.

A rooster crowed in the distance.

It was a different Peter who sat in the house two days later, on Sunday morning. Jesus was dead—crucified on a hill outside the city gates and buried in a borrowed tomb. Everything they had worked for, everything they had hoped for, was lost. All gone. All for nothing. He had said He was the Messiah!

When the woman knocked on the door, no one wanted to answer. Peter sat, his head in his hands, his spirit deflated. But the knocking persisted. "I've seen the Lord!" the woman shouted through the heavy wooden door. "The tomb—it's empty!"

Could it be true? Peter pushed past the others and ran all the way to the garden tomb. He could hardly believe his eyes: Somebody had rolled aside the huge stone at the entrance to the tomb. He flew down the steps into the musty tomb and saw the folded burial garment where the body once lay. Jesus had risen from the dead!

The next several weeks passed in a flurry. Jesus walked and talked with His disciples again, but only for a little while. He had to return to His Father in heaven, He said.

Gradually, the disciples returned to their old jobs. What else was there to do? Early one morning, Peter and the other fishermen struggled to catch fish, but the fish weren't biting. A man waved to them from the shore. "Try casting your nets on the other side of the boat," He called out. They did, and the catch was so big it threatened to burst their nets.

Peter's heart thudded in his chest. "It's the Lord!" he shouted, and dove into the water and swam to shore. There sat Jesus, casually frying fish over an open fire.

"Come and have breakfast," He said, a broad smile lighting His face.

They ate together, but the conversation dragged. Something was not right, and both men knew what it was.

"Peter, do you love Me?" Jesus asked.

"Yes, Lord, You know I love You," the burly disciple answered.

"Feed My lambs," Jesus said.

He paused and then said again, "Peter, do you truly love Me?"

"Yes, Lord, You know that I do."

"Take care of My sheep . . . Peter, do you love Me?"

Now Peter was confused. "Lord, You know all things; You know that I love You."

"Feed My sheep."

Three times Jesus asked, and three times Peter gave his confirmation. In that seaside breakfast for two, Jesus restored Peter's heart and revalidated him as a man—a man of God. One time for each denial.

The sound of a rooster crowing would never haunt Peter again.

ChaPter TEN

Witness
like a
JESUS
Freak

Jesus was waiting for them when they got there. The eleven disciples—the traitor Judas was dead at this point—had agreed to meet Him here on the mountain in Galilee. As they approached, they could tell from the look in His eyes that He had something important to say.

It was always that way with Jesus. After hanging around Him for three solid years, this ragtag band of men knew at a glance when the Master was about to say something profound. Something life changing. He never wasted words, and when His eyes blazed the way they did today, it meant something big was up.

As the men drew close to Him, Jesus scanned each of their faces. Now the blazing eyes held a look so full of love that the men had to glance away—embarrassed, vulnerable. It was as if He was imprinting their every feature on His memory.

"Master?" the leader of the group said, his unspoken question hanging in the air.

In response, Jesus opened His arms in a wide gesture of blessing. Then He spoke: "All authority in heaven and on earth has been given to Me. Therefore go and make disciples of all nations, baptizing them in the name of the Father and of the Son and of the Holy Spirit, and teaching them to obey everything I have commanded you."

He paused only a second before giving His final promise: "And surely I am with you always, to the very end of the age."

This was it, then—their "marching orders." Jesus was going back to the Father as He had said He must do. And now the disciples would be on their own, although not entirely. In a few weeks He would send the Helper, the Holy Spirit, although what that really meant they couldn't imagine right now.

As the disciples watched, Jesus blessed them one by one, calling each by name. Was He suddenly growing taller? No! He was rising off the ground, His arms still outstretched, His lips still moving. Those shining eyes were the last things the disciples saw before the cloud swallowed Him up, and He was gone.

Did Somebody Say "Good News"?

The Scriptures call the gospel Good News. That's not just a hokey nickname coined by some Bible-thumping Sunday school superintendent. Learning how a person can become a Jesus Freak is good news in the truest sense.

Imagine you're a pathologist, and after twenty years of research you've finally discovered a sure cure for cancer—every type of cancer. What would you do? You'd call *The New York Times*. You'd call Oprah. You'd schedule interviews with all the major TV networks. You'd hold seminars, passing on your knowledge to everyone of the medical community. Meanwhile, two-inch headlines would scream from the front pages of newspapers around the world: *Cure for Cancer Found!*

A cure for cancer? That's good news. A guarantee of eternal life? That's even better.

The Good News of the gospel means that anyone who abandons their own way of life and follows after Jesus will live with Him forever. Forget karma. Forget reincarnation. There really is life after death, but what you do with Jesus Christ here and now makes all the difference in what that life will be like. Through His death, He's paid for you to live a life more wonderful than words can describe. But for those who reject Him, life after death will be a living hell—an eternity stretching out before them, separated from God, their only companions other tormented souls and demonic spirits.

When Jesus delivered the Great Commission to His disciples, He was really talking to all Jesus Freaks. "Go into all nations and make disciples" can be translated "get involved in other people's lives." Make a difference. Keep talking about Jesus and the change He's made in your life. Tell everyone you can, any way you can.

Learning **HOW** a **person** can become a Jesus Freak is GOOD **news** in **the truest** SENSE.

Aren't you glad someone told you about the gospel? Whether you became a Jesus Freak through a friend, a pastor, an evangelist, a film, a song, a story, a poem, a television program, or any other means, someone had to put into words or images what being a Jesus Freak means. It took effort. It took action. And God promises that when we share His Word in any way, shape, or form, it will bear fruit. Souls will be saved. Lives will be changed. New Jesus Freaks will be "born" into the kingdom of God.

When you start digging—and start asking—it's amazing the answers you'll find. God can use just about anything to turn a person into a Jesus Freak. For Hudson Taylor, one of the greatest missionaries of all time, He used a gospel tract.

Taylor was a guy who dreamed big. At age five, he told friends he wanted to be a missionary to Asia. He had heard the stories of Paul's missionary journeys and imagined he'd do the same—reach thousands of people with the gospel. The only problem: Taylor wasn't actually converted to Christ until many years later.

His mother prayed that God would break through to her son. One day, while she was far from home, she felt a strong urging to stop and pray for him. She entered her room, locked the door, and didn't come out until she felt sure of Hudson's salvation.

Back at home, her seventeen-year-old son was bored, shuffling around the house with nothing to do. He wandered into his father's library and picked up some papers lying on the desk. A leaflet caught his eye. It started with an interesting story, so he kept reading. Later, Taylor would write, "Light was flashed into my soul by the Holy Spirit. There was nothing in the world to be done but to fall down on one's knees and [pray for salvation]."

After a brief stay in medical school, Taylor sailed for China in the mid 1860s. But he didn't have a fairytale time in Asia. Even though God brought him safely to his destination, once there he suffered from deep depression, homesickness, physical illness, financial crises, language barriers, and personality conflicts with other missionaries. Wanting to be accepted by the Chinese, he dyed his hair jet black and let it grow, wearing a long pigtail like the other men. As the years passed, he sank deeper into depression.

This time, God used the words of a friend to bolster Taylor's spirit. The friend wrote a letter urging Taylor to try ". . . abiding, not striving nor struggling." Christ Himself is "the only power for service; the only ground for unchanging joy," he continued.

Hudson Taylor said, "As I read, I saw it all. I looked to Jesus; and when I saw, oh, how the joy flowed. As to work, mine was never so plentiful or so difficult; but the weight and strain are gone."

At the time of Taylor's death, China Inland Mission—the organization he founded—had 800 missionaries in China. It still exists to this day and goes by the name Overseas Missionary Fellowship. OMF takes the gospel to twelve countries in East Asia, carrying on the vision of a little boy who dared to dream big.

From Greek to Freak

For Francis Schaeffer, God used a clerk's simple error to transform him into a Jesus Freak. Known as a missionary to the intellectuals of the mid-twentieth century, Schaeffer wrote the classic *How Should We Then Live?* But long before he earned that distinction, Schaeffer was a typical teenager, though one inclined toward deep thinking.

Reared in a non-religious home, Schaeffer had little knowledge of the Scriptures. When he was seventeen he took a job teaching English to a Russian immigrant. To aid his teaching, he went to a bookstore to buy an English grammar book. When he got home, he discovered the clerk had bagged the wrong book and instead had given him an introduction to Greek philosophy.

The book's heady content drew Schaeffer in. He devoured every word. But he found that the Greek philosophers offered no answers to the basic questions about the meaning of life: *Why are we here? How did we get here? Where do we go when we die? Is there a Great Being somewhere out there?*

Having heard the Bible's claim to hold the truth, he decided to read it cover to cover. By the time he reached Revelation, Francis Schaeffer was a changed man. God didn't require him to "dumb down" his sharp, intellectual mind. Instead, He used Schaeffer's gifts to reach other intellectuals. In 1955, Schaeffer and his wife, Edith, founded L'Abri Fellowship, a study and retreat center in Switzerland for students

Why are we HERE? How did we GET here? Where do we go when we die? Is THERE a Great Being somewhere out THERE?

and skeptics seeking answers to the great philosophical questions of life.

Anything Goes

God is not picky. He'll use any method it takes to win a soul to Jesus Christ. Here are several ways you can get the word out that He is alive and well on planet Earth!

- *Relational*. Many Jesus Freaks do this type of witnessing every day of their lives and may not even realize it. If so, more power to you...*really!* There's nothing like the story of a changed life to change another life. When asked, most people point to another human being as the single most important factor in their conversion to Christ. Don't hold out on others! God is waiting to draw them into His kingdom too, and He just may use you to accomplish it. Do you sense Him telling you to speak to that girl in your history class? Is the Spirit prodding you to pray for that man you see every day at the convenience store? Don't wait! Another soul may be hanging in the balance.

- *Letters*. Do you have a way with words? If writing comes more easily to you than speaking, why not write a letter to your non-Jesus Freak friends and relatives? That way they can think about your words long after you've written them. This is what the apostle Paul did to the Jesus Freaks of his day. He wrote letter after letter, encouraging them, correcting them, and gently guiding them along the Godly path.

- *Neighborhood club/small group.* Start a Bible reading group on your campus, or host a small group in your home. Spread the word around via e-mail, flyers, or the neighborhood grapevine. You can focus your group in a number of ways: reading spiritual classics, studying and discussing the Bible, worshipping God and encouraging each other, or a combination of all three. Maybe you, too, have an intellectual bent and want to provide a forum for thinkers—a place where skeptics can air their questions and dig for real answers.

- *Street evangelism.* If you're the bold type, find a busy part of town on a Saturday night and talk to people about Jesus. Many cities have a "hot spot"—a theater strip or club district. That's usually a great place to start.

- *The arts.* Once considered too avant-garde by the traditional church, the arts are now an accepted method of evangelism—and a very powerful one. Drama, dance, mime, comedy, clowning, and other art forms speak to people through a subtle, symbolic language. God gave us the arts. He gave us artistic talents and the desire to express them. What better way to use them than for His glory?

- *Gospel tracts.* If you're uncomfortable handing out tracts in person, try the subtle approach. Leave them in places where people are bound to bump into them—on car windshields, park benches, bus or /train seats, restaurant tabletops; in locker rooms, theaters, bathrooms, and Internet cafes. Do not leave a tract at a restaurant unless you also leave a very generous tip.

"Jesus does not promise that when we bless our enemies and do good to them they will not despise us and persecute us. They certainly will.

But not even that can hurt us or overcome us, so long as we pray for them. For if we pray for them, we are taking their distress and poverty, guilt and perdition upon ourselves, and pleading to God for them.

Every insult they utter only serves to bind us more closely to God and them. Their persecution of us only serves to bring them nearer to reconciliation with God and to further the triumphs of love.

It is only when one sees the anger and wrath of God hanging like grim realities over the head of one's enemies that one can know something of what it means to love them and forgive them."

Dietrich Bonhoeffer
Hanged in Nazi Germany
1945

The impression you make on another human being may be the thing that changes their eternity. Your story—your changed life—could be the missing piece to their puzzle. And once God crosses your path with theirs, a new future may be written in the Book of Life. Go ahead. Witness like a Jesus Freak!

Living like a Jesus Freak is a life of adventure. Sometimes it calls for huge personal sacrifice, at times even death. But Jesus Freak martyrs would no doubt give a unanimous answer if asked, "Was it worth it?"

A faith worth living for is a faith worth dying for.

What "tool" did God use to turn you into a
Jesus Freak?

How can you make yourself available to Him to be a
catalyst for someone else's salvation?

You want your friends to have what you have. How
can you tell them about this new life?

Ask God to give you the opportunity to talk about
Jesus to three people this week. Ask for the boldness
to share your own story of how you became a Jesus
Freak.

Jesus Freaks Around You Now

Smiling at Her Torturer
Liuba Ganevskaya
U.S.S.R., 1970s

Enough is enough, Liuba Ganevskaya said to herself. *I will not receive the blows with meekness anymore. Tonight, if they begin again, I will tell the guard to his face that he is a criminal.*

Liuba, arrested for her faith by the Russian Communists, was kept in a solitary cell, starved, and beaten. Still, she had not denied Jesus or revealed the names of other believers. Like so many others, she had patiently suffered for the sake of the gospel.

She promised herself that tonight would be different.

But that night, when the guard insulted her with foul words and was just about to start beating her, she somehow saw him differently.

She noticed, for the first time, that he was as tired of beating her as she was tired of being beaten. She was worn out from lack of sleep, and so was he. He was as desperate over not getting any information from her as she was about suffering for refusing to betray her friends.

A voice told her, "He is so much like you. You are both caught in the same drama of life." Stalin, the chief Communist dictator, killed thousands of God's children, but he also killed 10,000 officers of his own secret police. Three successive heads of the police—Yagoda, Yezhov, and Beria—were shot by their comrades, just like the Christians they had persecuted!

"You and your torturer pass through the same vale of tears."

Liuba looked up at the guard, who had already lifted the whip to beat her. She smiled.

Stunned, he asked, "Why do you smile?"

She replied, "I don't see you the way a mirror would show you right now. I see you as you surely once were, a beautiful, innocent child. We are the same age. We might have been playmates.

"I see you, too, as I hope you will be. There was once a persecutor worse than you named Saul of Tarsus. He became an apostle and a saint."

The torturer put down his whip.

She continued, "What burden so weighs on you that it drives you to the madness of beating a person who has done you no harm?"

He had no answer. The torturer left that day a changed man.[18]

Jesus Freaks in the Bible

Joseph: The Model Mentor

Joseph could have made a great CEO. He was an excellent judge of character, and knew just where a person should be plugged in to maximize his strengths. Joseph saw good in all men, and was more than willing to give someone a second chance.

It was this willingness that got him "fired" from his biggest, best-known gig.

Exactly when Joseph came to faith in Jesus is not known. But we do know that he met up with the early church fathers shortly after the Day of Pentecost. He believed so strongly in the Good News message the apostles were sharing that he sold some real estate he owned and gave the money to the church. He then threw himself in headlong to mentoring believers who also wished to share the Good News of Jesus.

One of the young men Joseph took under his wings was a suspect new believer by the name of Paul. Paul, or Saul, as he had previously been known, wanted to share about his new-found faith, but many in the church were still afraid of him. After all, Paul had spent considerable time and energy rooting out believers and turning them over to the authorities for punishment. But Joseph saw that enthusiasm had not abated; it had simply shifted gears from tormenting followers of Jesus to wanting to recruit new followers. Joseph gave Paul a chance. Soon, Joseph and Paul were inseparable, traveling

the known-world telling about the saving power of
Jesus, and seeing God perform healing miracles. Paul
was no longer feared by the church—as a matter of
fact, he became one of the pillars of the first century
body of believers.

On one of their journeys, Joseph and Paul
decided to take along a young believer by the name
of John Mark. Mark was eager to experience the
miracles Joseph and Paul had seen on their previous
trips. But when the way got hard, when their lives
began to be threatened because of the Good News
message they were preaching, Mark's enthusiasm
faded. One morning he said he had had enough, and
set out for home.

One a subsequent trip, Mark said he wanted a
second chance. He was ready to lay down his life this
time if necessary. But Paul was not willing to give
Mark a second opportunity. He and Joseph got into a
heated exchange—and in the end, Paul and Joseph
went their separate ways.

We do not hear directly about Joseph from this
point, as the author of the book of Acts follows the
adventures of Paul from here on out. But we can
assume that Joseph kept up with his mentoring of
Mark, as later in Paul's life he sent for Timothy to
send Mark to him, for "Mark can be very helpful to
me" (2 Timothy 4:11 CEV). Joseph's encouragement
of Mark eventually proved valuable to Paul.

Joseph was also an encourager. The other disciples saw this attribute in Joseph early on. And, like
friends often do, they gave Joseph a nickname, the

name by which we know him, the name that means "one who encourages others."

His given name was Joseph. But we know him as Barnabas. And now when you read the Gospel of Mark, the earliest account of the life of Jesus, you will know he had a mentor who stuck with him when others gave up. Barnabas is our model of what a mentor should be.

Endnotes

1. *Merriam-Webster's Collegiate Dictionary*, 10th ed., s.v. "freak."

2. From *Jesus Freaks* by dc Talk and Voice of the Martyrs (Albury Publishing: Tulsa, OK, 1999).

3. From *The Hiding Place* (reissue edition) by Corrie ten Boom (Bantam Books: NY, 1984).

4. From *Jesus Freaks*.

5. From *The Paraclete Letter*, July 2, 2001.

6. *Merriam-Webster's Collegiate Dictionary*, 10th ed., s.v. "fervent".

7. From *Jesus Freaks*.

8. From *Jesus Freaks*.

9. Story excerpted from *Front Porch Tales* by Philip Gulley (Multnomah Books: Sisters, OR, 1997).

10. From *Out of the Saltshaker & Into the World* by Rebecca Manley Pippert (InterVarsity Press: Downers Grove, IL, 1999).

11. From *Sunday Sermons* (September/October 1983), Voicings: Pleasantville, NJ.

12. From *Jesus Freaks*.

13. From *Jesus Freaks*.

14. From *Jesus Freaks*.

15. *Merriam-Webster's Collegiate Dictionary*, 10th ed.

16. From *Jesus Freaks*.

17. From *Jesus Freaks*.

18. From *Jesus Freaks*.

About dc Talk

Toby McKeehan   **Michael Tait**   **Kevin Max**

Since releasing their album *Jesus Freak*, dc Talk has emerged as a leader in the pursuit of melding rock 'n' roll with provocative questions of faith.

Although various rock predecessors have examined spiritual issues—U2, Van Morrison, and Bob Dylan immediately come to mind—dc Talk has taken the notion to new lengths, both in commercial terms and depth of artistic exploration. Numerous Dove Awards, three Grammy Awards, two platinum albums, one gold album, and two gold-certified long-form videos attest to the group's ability to bridge the gap between religious and secular audiences.

Toby, Michael, and Kevin first met in the mid-80's while attending college in Virginia. After relocating to Nashville, dc Talk released a series of increasingly ambitious—and successful—albums, beginning with their self-titled 1989 debut; followed by their gold-certified 1990 sophomore album *Nu Thang*; the platinum-certified 1992 opus *Free at Last*; 1995's *Jesus Freak*, a platinum-plus watershed that afforded the group more mainstream success than ever before; and 1998's *Supernatural*, which reflects the maturity and sophistication of their latest stage of development and growth.

In 2000, while on a hiatus from recording and traveling, the group released *intermission*, a greatest hits recording that also included two brand-new songs. For the year 2001, the group will collectively release four new CD's. Each member has released a solo album— and a dc Talk release entitled *Solo*, which includes two songs from each of the guys' upcoming solo albums.

Their first book, *Jesus Freaks*, has had a tremendous impact. The stories of true Jesus Freaks have challenged young people to stand up for their Savior. Upcoming *Jesus Freaks* books will encourage those who were touched by *Jesus Freaks* to go deeper in their relationship with the Lord.

Fear God, Not Man

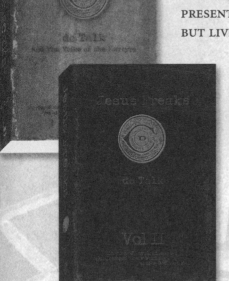

THE FIRST STEP TO BECOME A JESUS FREAK IS TO REALIZE THAT YOUR LIFE IS NOT YOUR OWN, BUT GOD'S. *JESUS FREAKS* BOOKS TELL THE STORIES OF MARTYRS AND REVOLUTIONARIES, PAST AND PRESENT WHO NOT ONLY MADE THAT DECISION BUT LIVED, STOOD, AND DIED BY IT.

Jesus Freaks by dc Talk and The Voice of the Martyrs
Their voices, calling down through history, will change you forever.

Jesus Freaks: Vol II by dc Talk
These revolutionaries show that it only takes one person to change the world.

Promises for a Jesus Freak by dc Talk
Wisdom straight from the Bible selected especially for Jesus Freaks

Live Like a Jesus Freak by dc Talk
Hard-hitting application for the lessons of *Jesus Freaks*

Jesus Freak Journal by dc Talk
A private place to journal your growing faith with God